C000149421

The South Carolina Coast

must SEES

Chief Editor	Cynthia Clayton Ochterbeck
Senior Editor	M. Linda Lee
Writer	M. Linda Lee
Contributing Writer	Martha Hunt
Production Coordinator	Allison M. Simpson
Cartography	Peter Wrenn; MapQuest
Photo Editor	Brigitta L. House
Proofreader	Margo Browning
Documentation	Doug Rogers
Typesetting	Octavo Design and Production
	Apopka, Florida
Cover Design	Paris Venise Design
	Paris, 17e
Printing and Binding	Banta Book Group
	Spanish Fork, UT

Michelin North America
One Parkway South
Greenville, SC 29615
USA
800-423-0485
www.michelin-us.com
email: TheGreenGuide-us@us.michelin.com

Special Sales:

For information regarding bulk sales, customized editions and premium sales, please
contact our Customer Service Departments:

USA – 800-423-0485   **Canada** – 800-361-8236

Manufacture française des pneumatiques Michelin
Société en commandite par actions au capital de 304 000 000 EUR
Place des Carmes-Déchaux – 63 Clermont-Ferrand (France)
R.C.S. Clermont-FD B 855 800 507

Note to the reader:

While every effort is made to ensure that all information in this guide is correct and up-
to-date, Michelin Travel Publications (Michelin North America, Inc.) accepts no liability
for any direct, indirect or consequential losses howsoever caused so far as such can be
excluded by law.

Admission prices listed for sights in this guide are for a single adult, unless otherwise
specified.

Welcome to the South Carolina Coast

Table of Contents

The Must Sees

Table of Contents

THE MICHELIN STARS

For more than 75 years, travelers have used the Michelin stars to take the guesswork out of planning a trip. Our star-rating system helps you make the best decision on where to go, what to do, and what to see. A three-star rating means it's one of the "absolutelys"; two stars means it's one of the "should sees"; and one star says it's one of the "sees" – a must if you have the time.

★★★   Absolutely Must See
★★   Really Must See
★   Must See

Sights listed below are located in South Carolina unless otherwise specified.

Three-Star Sights

Charleston★★★
Charleston Historic District★★★
Drayton Hall★★★
Fort Sumter National Monument★★★
Nathaniel Russell House★★★
Middleton Place★★★
Middleton Place Gardens★★★

Two-Star Sights

Aiken-Rhett House★★
The Battery★★
Brookgreen Gardens★★
Circular Congregational Church★★
Cumberland Island National Seashore★★ (GA)
Edmondston-Alston House★★
Factors Walk★★ (GA)
The Grand Strand★★
Heyward-Washington House★★
Jekyll Island★★ (GA)
Jekyll Island National
   Historic Landmark District★★ (GA)
Kiawah Island★★
Magnolia Plantation★★
Old City Market★★
Owens-Thomas House★★ (GA)
Patriots Point Naval & Maritime Museum★★
Savannah★★ (GA)

Savannah Historic District★★ (GA)
South Carolina Aquarium★★
Spoleto USA Festival★★
USS Yorktown★★

One-Star Sights

Audubon Swamp Garden★
Andrew Low House★ (GA)
Beaufort★
Cathedral of St. John the Baptist★ (GA)
Charles Pinckney National Historic Site★
Charleston Museum★
Dock Street Theatre★
First African Baptist Church★ (GA)
First (Scots) Presbyterian Church★
French Huguenot Church★
Forsyth Park★ (GA)
Fort Frederica National Monument★ (GA)
Fort Moultrie★
Fort Pulaski National Monument★ (GA)
Gibbes Museum of Art★
Golden Isles★ (GA)
Hilton Head Island★
Huntington Beach State Park★
Hunting Island State Park★
Isaiah Davenport House★ (GA)
Isle of Palms★
Joseph Manigault House★
King Street Shopping★
The Lowcountry Coast★
Market Hall★
Mercer House★ (GA)
Myrtle Beach★
Myrtle Beach State Park★
Old Exchange Building★
Piccolo Spoleto★
Ships of the Sea Maritime Museum★ (GA)
St. Michael's Episcopal Church★
St. Simons Island★ (GA)
Telfair Academy of Arts and Sciences★ (GA)
Waterfront Park★
White Point Gardens★
Wild Dunes★

Calendar of Events

Listed below is a selection of the most popular annual events in Charleston, the Carolina Coast, and Savannah and the Golden Isles in Georgia. Please note that dates may vary year to year. *For more detailed information, contact the convention and visitors bureaus listed on p 10 and p 17.*

January

Lowcountry Oyster Festival   843-577-4030
Boone Hall Plantation, Mt. Pleasant, SC
     www.charlestonrestaurantassociation.com/
          oysterfestival.htm

Taste of Savannah   912-232-1223
Savannah International Trade & Convention Center
     Savannah, GA   www.tourismleadershipcouncil.com

February

Black Heritage Festival   912-236-4898
Various locations, Savannah, GA   www.savstate.edu

Native Islander Gullah Celebration   843-682-3742
Hilton Head Island, SC   www.gullahcelebration.com

March

Canadian American Days Festival   843-626-7444
Myrtle Beach, SC
     www.mbchamber.com/cvb/events/canam/index.htm

Festival of Houses & Gardens   843-722-3405
Historic District, Charleston, SC
     (mid-Mar–mid-Apr)   www.historiccharleston.org

Saint Patrick's Day Celebration   912-644-6400
Various locations, Savannah, GA
                                    www.savannahvisit.com

April

Cooper River Bridge Run   843-792-6611
Charleston, SC   www.bridgerun.com

Family Circle Cup Tennis Tournament   800-677-2293
Family Circle Tennis Center
     Charleston, SC   www.familycirclecup.com

Grand Strand Fishing Rodeo   843-626-7444
Myrtle Beach, SC (Apr 1–Oct 31)
     www.mbchamber.com/cvb/events/fishrodeo

Legends of Golf, PGA Champions Tour   912-236-1333
Westin Savannah Harbor Golf Resort & Spa
     Savannah, GA   www.pgatour.com

Sidewalk Arts Festival   912-236-1333
Forsyth Park, Savannah, GA   www.scad.edu

May

Charleston Maritime Festival   843-856-0392
Charleston Maritime Center, 10 Wharfside St.
               www.charlestonmaritimefestival.com

Savannah Seafood Festival   912-234-0295
River St., Savannah, GA   www.savriverstreet.com

Piccolo Spoleto   843-724-7305
Various locations, Charleston, SC
     (late May–early June)   www.piccolospoleto.org

Spoleto   843-579-3100
Various locations, Charleston, SC
     (late May–early June)   www.spoletousa.org

Calendar of Events

June

Annual Sun Fun Festival 800-356-3016
Myrtle Beach, SC   www.myrtlebeachinfo.com

July

Beaufort Water Festival 843-524-3163
Henry C. Chambers Waterfront Park
   Beaufort, SC   www.beaufortsc.org

Fourth of July on the Waterfront 912-234-0295
River St., Savannah, GA   www.savriverstreet.com

Patriots Point 4th of July Blast 843-884-2727
Patriots Point, Mt. Pleasant, SC   www.patriotspoint.org

August

Seafood & Music Festival 800-868-2322
North Beach parking lot, across from lighthouse
   Tybee Island, GA   www.tybeevisit.com

September

Fall Candlelight Tour of 800-968-8175
   Homes & Gardens   www.preservationsociety.org
Historic District, Charleston, SC

Festival Hispano 843-795-4386
Wannamaker Park, Charleston, SC   www.ccprc.com

Savannah Jazz Festival 912-232-2222
Forsyth Park, Savannah, GA   www.coastaljazz.com

October

Beaufort Shrimp Festival 843-524-3163
Waterfront Park, Beaufort, SC   www.beaufortsc.org

Oktoberfest 912-234-0295
River St., Savannah, GA   www.savriverstreet.com

Surf Kayak Rodeo 843-795-4386
Folly Beach Fishing Pier, SC   www.ccprc.com

Taste of Charleston 843-577-4030
Boone Hall Plantation, Mt. Pleasant, SC
   www.charlestonlowcountry.com

November

Penn Center Heritage Days 843-838-2432
Penn Center
   St. Helena Island, SC   www.penncenter.com

Plantation Days at Middleton Place 800-782-3608
Middleton Place, Charleston   www.middletonplace.org

December

Holiday Festival of Lights 843-762-2172
James Island County Park   www.ccprc.com
   James Island, SC

Holiday Parade of Boats 843-724-7414
Charleston Harbor   www.christmasincharleston.com

Holiday Tour of Homes 912-236-8362
Historic District, Savannah, GA

   www.dnaholidaytour.net

Must Know: Practical Information

Area Codes

To call between different area codes, dial 1 + area code + seven-digit number. It's not necessary to use the area code to make a local call.

Charleston, Kiawah, Isle of Palms, Myrtle Beach and Hilton Head: **843**
Savannah and the Golden Isles of Georgia: **912**

PLANNING YOUR TRIP

Before you go, contact the following organizations to obtain maps and information about sightseeing, accommodations, travel packages and seasonal events.

Charleston Area Convention and Visitors Bureau

423 King St., Charleston, SC 29403
843-853-8000 or 800-774-0006; www.charlestoncvb.com

Visitor Centers

All visitor centers below are closed Jan 1, Thanksgiving Day & Dec 25.

Charleston Visitor Reception Center

375 Meeting St.
843-853-8000; www.charlestoncvb.com
Open Mar–Oct daily 8:30am–5:30pm.
Rest of the year daily 8:30am–5pm.

Kiawah Island Visitor Center

22 Beachwalker Dr., Kiawah Island
843-853-8000; www.charlestoncvb.com
Open year-round daily 9am–5pm.

Mt. Pleasant–Isle of Palms Visitor Center

311 Johnnie Dodds Blvd., in Bridge Way
Village, Mt. Pleasant
843-853-8000; www.charlestoncvb.com.
Open year-round daily 9am–5:50pm.

North Charleston Visitor Center

3107 Firestone Rd., North Charleston
843-853-8000; www.charlestoncvb.com
Open year-round daily 9am–5:50pm.

Web Sites

Here are some additional Web sites to help you plan your trip:
www.charlestonlowcountry.com
www.discovercharleston.com
www.accesscharleston.com
www.charleston.com
www.charleston.net

Forever Charleston

If time permits, this half-hour video, shown at the Charleston Visitor Reception Center, makes a great introduction to the Holy City. *Forever Charleston* tells the city's story in Charlestonians' own words, using images from a host of sources *($2 adults, $1 children under age 11).*

In The News

Charleston's main daily newspaper is the *Post and Courier (www.charleston.net); Preview*, the arts and entertainment supplement, is published every Thursday. Other periodicals include: *The Chronicle*, an African-American weekly; the *Charleston City Paper*, published weekly *(www.charlestoncitypaper.com); Skirt*, a free monthly magazine for women *(www.skirtmag.com);* and *Charleston Magazine (www.charleston mag.com).*

TIPS FOR SPECIAL VISITORS

Disabled Travelers – Federal law requires that businesses (including hotels and restaurants) provide access for the disabled, devices for the hearing impaired, and designated parking spaces. For further information, contact the Society for Accessible Travel and Hospitality (SATH), 347 Fifth Ave., Suite 610, New York NY 10016 *(212-447-7284; www.sath.org)*.

All national parks have facilities for the disabled, and offer free or discounted passes. For details, contact the National Park Service *(Office of Public Inquiries, P.O. Box 37127, Room 1013, Washington, DC 20013-7127; 202-208-4747; ww.nps.gov)*.

Passengers who will need assistance with train or bus travel should give advance notice to Amtrak *(800-872-7245 or 800-523-6590/TDD; www.amtrak.com)* or Greyhound *(800-752-4841 or 800-345-3109/TDD; www.greyhound.com)*. Reservations for hand-controlled rental cars should be made in advance with the rental company.

Local Lowdown – The following organizations provide detailed information about access for the disabled in Charleston:

• The brochure *REHAB's Accessibility Guide to Greater Charleston* is available at the Visitor Reception Center *(opposite)*.

• Check the **Charleston Area Convention and Visitors Bureau** Web site *(www.charlestoncvb.com)* for information about attractions that offer access for the disabled.

• Contact the **Charleston Area Regional Transit Authority (CARTA)** for information about disabled access to public transportation *(843-724-7420; www.ridecarta.com)*.

• **South Carolina Handicapped Services Information**: 803-777-5732.

Senior Citizens – Many hotels, attractions and restaurants offer discounts to visitors age 62 or older (proof of age may be required). The AARP (formerly the American Association of Retired Persons) offers discounts to its members *(601 E St. NW, Washington, DC 20049; 202-434-2277; www.aarp.com)*.

Important Numbers	
Emergency (Police/Ambulance/Fire Department, 24hrs)	911
Police *(non-emergency, Mon–Fri 9am–6pm)*	843-554-5700
Poison Control	800-922-1117
Medical Referral:	
Bon Secours-St. Francis/Roper Hospital	843-402-2273
	800-863-2273
Charleston County Medical Society	843-577-3613
East Cooper Regional Medical Center	843-884-7031
	800-311-4803
Medical University of South Carolina	843-792-1414
Trident Healthfinders	843-797-3463
Dental Emergencies: North Charleston Dental Center	843-744-2610
24-hour Pharmacy: Walgreens, 907 Folly Rd	843-795-2294

Must Know: Practical Information

WHEN TO GO

With its sub-tropical climate, the South Carolina Coast is a great place to visit year-round. The best times to come, weather-wise—spring and fall—are also the most crowded. Spring is a lovely time of year in Charleston; this is when the popular Festival of Homes and Gardens *(see p 86)* is held, and also when the famous Spoleto festival takes place *(see Performing Arts)*. Summers in the Low-country are hot and humid—sometimes oppressively so—but that doesn't stop sun-seekers from packing the beaches up and down the coast. In fall, the beach crowds go home and golfers turn out in droves to enjoy the crisp, clear weather on area courses. Winters are usually mild—it's not uncommon to have 60-degree days in January. Hotel rates in Charleston plummet this time of year.

Seasonal Temperatures in Charleston

	Jan	Apr	July	Oct
Avg. high	58°F / 14°C	74°F / 23°C	89°F / 32°C	76°F / 24°C
Avg. low	40°F / 4°C	57°F / 14°C	73°F / 23°C	60°F /16°C

Getting Hitched

Thinking about getting married? With its lovely historic homes, lush gardens and beautiful beaches, Charleston makes an ideal setting for a wedding. Get all the information you need, from hair stylists to party halls, in the *Charleston Area Wedding Guide,* available from the Charleston Area Convention and Visitors Bureau *(for details, contact the Sales Department: 800-868-8118, ext. 3072; www.charlestonweddingguide.com).*

GETTING THERE

By Air – Most major airlines service **Charleston International Airport (CHS)**, located 12 miles west of downtown off I-526 *(5500 International Blvd., 843-767-1100; www.chs-airport.com).*

A taxi from the airport to downtown costs approximately $20–$22. A more economical alternative, shuttles are available through Airport Ground Transportation, located outside baggage claim. Shuttle service to downtown is $10 per person.

By Train – Amtrak provides service to Charleston; the rail station is located at 4565 Gaynor Avenue in North Charleston *(843-744-8264)*. For rates, schedules and reservations, contact Amtrak: 800-872-7245 or www.amtrak.com.

By Bus – For departures or arrivals by bus, the Greyhound Terminal is located in North Charleston *(3610 Dorchester Rd.; 843-747-5341)*. For rates, schedules and reservations, contact Greyhound: 800-231-2222 or 843-744-4247; www.greyhound.com.

By Car – Charleston lies about 52 miles southeast of I-95, the main north-south corridor on the East Coast. From I-95, or approaching from farther west, take I-26 directly to the city.

GETTING AROUND

By Car – Charleston is not laid out in a neat grid, but at 5.2 square miles, the peninsula on which the Historic District is located isn't difficult to navigate. Meeting Street and East Bay Street are the main access points from the interstate highways. King Street, which is one-way going toward the Battery on the other side of Calhoun Street, is one of the main commercial thoroughfares. As you're driving, be cautious around the ever-present horse-drawn carriages that take visitors through the historic downtown. Use of a seat belt is required in South Carolina, and child safety seats are mandatory for children under 6 years and 80 pounds.

The New Cooper River Bridge

Opened to traffic in 1929, the original 2.71-mile truss bridge over the Cooper River connected the city of Charleston to Mt. Pleasant and the barrier islands just north. Another span was added next to the aging bridge in 1966. Today the original bridge is considered obsolete, but never fear—a new span is currently being constructed. Scheduled to open in summer 2005, the Arthur Ravenel, Jr. Bridge will hover 570 feet above the river and provide eight lanes for traffic, plus a pedestrian/bicycle lane. The signature diamond-tower design of North America's longest cable-stay bridge incorporates state-of-the-art seismic technology.

Parking – Metered street parking is available in Charleston, but it can be scarce, especially in high season and during business hours. Parking garages are a better bet; you'll find them located at Aquarium Wharf and throughout the downtown area.

By Foot – Walking is the best way to get around the Historic District. Meandering down the streets is a great way to take in the stunning architecture and peek into the hidden private gardens. Although the area is generally very safe and heavily touristed, as in any city, you should beware of your surroundings when walking at night.

Charleston Walking Tours

Just got into Charleston and don't know where to start? Taking a walking tour makes a great introduction to the city. There are many to choose from, and prices vary, depending on the subject and length of the tour. Below is a sampling to get you off on the right foot:

Architectural Walking Tours of Charleston – 843-893-2327 or 800-931-7761. www.architecturalwalkingtoursofcharleston.com. Tours depart from the Meeting Street Inn, 173 Meeting St.

Charleston Strolls – 843-766-2080. www.charlestonstrolls.com. Tours depart from various Historic District hotels.

The Original Charleston Walks – 843-577-3800. www.charlestonwalks.com. Tours depart from the ticket office at 58 ½ Broad St.

Tour Charleston – 843-723-1670 or 800-854-1670. www.tourcharleston.com. Tours depart from the Circular Fountain at the entrance to Waterfront Park (at the end of Vendue Range).

Must Know: Practical Information

By Public Transportation – **Charleston Area Regional Transit Authority (CARTA)** runs an extensive network of public buses and trolleys linking downtown with West Ashley and North Charleston *(843-724-7420; www.ridecarta.com)*. Bus stops are marked with signs. Fare is $1.25 for a one-way trip *(exact change required; transfers cost 25¢)*. Children under age 6 ride free with a paying passenger.

You can purchase bus passes from CARTA bus or DASH trolley drivers, at the Visitor Reception Center *(375 Meeting St.)*, at all area Piggly Wiggly grocery stores, and at the CARTA office *(36 John St)*.

• All-day pass – $4
• 10-ride pass – $10
• 40-ride pass –$35

Charleston Pedicab

26 Cumberland St. 843-577-7088 (call for cabs between 4:30pm and when bars close). www.charlestonpedicab.com.

"Saving soles" is what Charleston Pedicab is all about. You'll see their open bicycle-powered rickshaw-like contraptions all over the Historic District. If you're tired of trekking the city's streets, catch a ride on one of these unique vehicles; the carts can carry 2 to 3 people. They'll even transport your wedding guests—or the bride and groom—to the church on time!

DASH Trolleys – Antique-looking green DASH trolleys operate one route between the South Carolina Aquarium, the Visitor Reception Center on Meeting Street, and the College of Charleston *($1.25; for schedules, call 843-747-0922)*.

By Taxi –The major cab companies in town are: **Express Cab** *(843-577-8816; $4 downtown flat rate; prices for other routes vary depending on destination)*, **Metro Cab** *(843-572-5083; $1.65/mile)*, and **Yellow Cab** *(843-577-6565; $3, then $1.25/mile)*.

FOREIGN VISITORS

Visitors from outside the US can obtain information from the Charleston Convention and Visitors Bureau *(www.cvb.org)* or from the US embassy or consulate in their country of residence. For a complete list of American consulates and embassies abroad, visit the US State Department Bureau of Consular Affairs listing on the Internet at: *http://travel.state.gov/links.html*.

Entry Requirements – Travelers entering the United States under the Visa Waiver Program (VWP) must have a machine-readable passport. Any traveler without a machine-readable passport will be required to obtain a visa before entering the US. Citizens of VWP countries are permitted to enter the US for general business or tourist purposes for a maximum of 90 days without needing a visa. Requirements for the Visa Waiver Program can be found at the Department of State's Visa Services Web site *(http://travel.state.gov/vwp.html)*.

All citizens of non-participating countries must have a visitor's visa. Upon entry, nonresident foreign visitors must present a valid passport and a round-trip transportation ticket. Canadian citizens are not required to present a passport or visa, but they must present a valid picture ID and proof of citizenship. Naturalized Canadian citizens should carry their citizenship papers.

US Customs – All articles brought into the US must be declared at the time of entry. Prohibited items: plant material; firearms and ammunition (if not for sporting purposes); meat or poultry products. For information, contact the US Customs Service, 1300 Pennsylvania Ave. NW, Washington, DC 20229 *(202-354-1000; www.cbp.gov)*.

Money and Currency Exchange – Visitors can exchange currency downtown at **Bank of America** *(544 King St.; 843-720-4913)* and **American Express Travel Service** at **Abbot & Hill Travel** *(10 Carriage Lane; 843-556-9051)*. For cash transfers, **Western Union** *(800-325-6000; www.westernunion.com)* has agents throughout the Charleston area. Banks, stores, restaurants and hotels accept travelers' checks with picture identification. To report a lost or stolen credit card: **American Express** *(800-528-4800)*; **Diners Club** *(800-234-6377)*; **MasterCard** *(800-307-7309)*; **Visa** *(800-336-8472)*.

Driving in the US – Visitors bearing valid driver's licenses issued by their country of residence are not required to obtain an International Driver's License. Drivers must carry vehicle registration and/or rental contract, and proof of automobile insurance at all times. Gasoline is sold by the gallon (1 gal=3.78 liters). Vehicles in the US are driven on the right-hand side of the road.

Electricity – Voltage in the US is 120 volts AC, 60 Hz. Foreign-made appliances may need AC adapters (available at specialty travel and electronics stores) and North American flat-blade plugs.

Taxes and Tipping – Prices displayed in the US do not include the Charleston sales tax of 6%, which is not reimbursable (1% sales-tax discount is given to citizens age 85 and older), or the hotel tax of 12%. It is customary to give a small gift of money—a tip—for services rendered, to waiters (15–20% of bill), porters ($1 per bag), hotel housekeeping staff ($1 per day) and cab drivers (15% of fare).

Measurement Equivalents

Degrees Fahrenheit	95°	86°	77°	68°	59°	50°	41°	32°	23°	14°
Degrees Celsius	35°	30°	25°	20°	15°	10°	5°	0°	-5°	-10°

1 inch = 2.5 centimeters   1 foot = 30.48 centimeters
1 mile = 1.6 kilometers   1 pound = 0.45 kilograms
1 quart = 0.9 liters   1 gallon = 3.78 liters

Time Zone

Charleston is located in the Eastern Time Zone (the same time zone as New York City), five hours behind Greenwich Mean Time.

ACCOMMODATIONS
For a list of suggested accommodations, see Must Stay.

Hotel Reservation Services

Historic Charleston Bed & Breakfast – *843-722-6606 or 800-743-3583. www.historiccharlestonbedandbreakfast.com*. For lodging in private homes in historic Charleston, this organization represents more than 50 bed-and-breakfast inns.

Must Know: Practical Information

Lowcountry Reservation Service – Located at the Visitor Reception Center (375 Meeting St.), this service offers in-person, same-day reservations for area hotels—often at a discount. No phone calls, please.

Hostels

A no-frills, inexpensive alternative to hotels, hostels are a great choice for budget travelers and students.

Charleston's Historic Hostel and Inn – 194 St. Philip St. 843-853-0846. Set near the shops and restaurants on King Street, the 1825 home offers both private ($40) and dorm-style ($19) rooms. Amenities include breakfast, Internet access, and DVD movies each night.

Not So Hostel – 156 Spring St. 843-722-8383. www.not-so-hostel.com. $19/night. Located outside the Historic District in a residential area downtown, this complex of three mid-19C houses contains air-conditioned dorm and private rooms with shared baths and kitchen. Breakfast and off-street parking are included in the rate.

Major hotel and motel chains with locations on the South Carolina Coast include:

Property	Phone	Web site
Best Western	800-780-7234	www.bestwestern.com
Comfort & Clarion Inns	877-424-6423	www.choicehotels.com
Days Inn	800-329-7466	www.daysinn.com
Hampton Inn	800-426-7866	www.hamptoninn.com
Hilton	800-774-1500	www.hilton.com
Holiday Inn	800-465-4329	www.holiday-inn.com
Sheraton	888-625-5144	www.sheraton.com
Radisson	888-201-1718	www.radisson.com
Ramada	800-228-2828	www.ramada.com
Westin	888-625-5144	www.westin.com

Accommodations at a Discount

Looking for a bargain? Try coming to Charleston mid-week in the summer. If you don't mind the sweltering heat and humidity, you can often find great room rates at some of city's upscale hotels.

If you're a golfer, be sure to ask about golf packages when you make your hotel reservations. Many accommodations along the coast will offer good rates that include a round or two at your choice of links.

SPECTATOR SPORTS

As a small city, Charleston doesn't have any professional sports teams, but it does offer a year-round calendar of sporting events, nonetheless. For more information on area sports, check out the Web site for the **Charleston Metro Sports Council**: www.sportscouncil.org.

Sport/Team	Venue	Info	Tickets/Web site
Class-A Baseball Charleston River Dogs	Joseph P. Riley Jr. Park	843-723-7241	843-577-3647 www.riverdogs.com
AA League/ECHL Hockey South Carolina Stingrays	North Charleston Coliseum	843-744-2248	877-843-7297 www.stingrayshockey.com
A-League Soccer Charleston Battery	Blackbaud Stadium, Daniel Island	843-971-4625	www.charlestonbattery.com

VISITING SAVANNAH AND THE GOLDEN ISLES

Before you go, contact the following organizations to obtain maps and information about sightseeing, accommodations, travel packages, recreational opportunities and seasonal events.

Savannah Convention and Visitors Bureau
101 E. Bay St., in the Historic District
912-644-6401 or 877-728-2662; www.savannah-visit.com

Brunswick and the Golden Isles Convention and Visitors Bureau
4 Glynn Ave., Brunswick, GA 315220
912-265-0620 or 800-933-2627; www.bgivb.com

Getting There – Several major airlines service **Savannah/Hilton Head International Airport (SAV)**, located 10 miles north of downtown, off I-95 *(400 Airways Ave.; 912-964-0514; www.savannahairport.com)*.

Two major airports provide service to Georgia's Golden Isles: **Savannah/Hilton Head International Airport** *(85mi north of Sea Island via I-95)* and **Jacksonville International Airport (JAX)**, located 70 miles south of Sea Island off I-95 *(2400 Yankee Clipper Dr., Jacksonville, FL; 904-741-4902; www.jaxairports.org)*. Little **Brunswick Golden Isles Airport** *(500 Connole St., Brunswick, GA; 912-265-2070; www.glynncountyairports.com)* is served by Atlantic Southeast Airlines and Delta Connection.

Getting There By Car – From the north or south, you can reach Savannah and the Golden Isles via I-95, the main north-south corridor along the East Coast. From the west, you can get to Savannah via I-16, which intersects with I-75 in Macon, Georgia. If you're headed to the Historic Downtown area, stay on I-16; it takes you straight into town.

Web Sites

Here are some additional Web sites to help you plan your trip:
www.savannahchamber.com
www.tybeevisit.com
www.coastalgeorgiaexperience.com

The South Carolina Coast

Southern Charm: The South Carolina Coast

Thoughts of the South Carolina Coast inevitably bring to mind palmetto trees and moss-draped live oaks, broad stretches of pale sand, the multitude of amusements of Myrtle Beach, and the handsome city of Charleston, where the area's history began.

Anchoring the coast on a narrow peninsula of land where the Ashley and Cooper rivers converge, Charleston was born in 1670 when a group of English colonists landed on the western bank of the Ashley River. The swampy settlement they named Charles Towne (after King Charles II; *see sidebar below*) was so plagued by disease and hunger during its first decade that the colonists moved the town in 1680 to a better location on the peninsula across the river.

Charles Towne's new location, surrounded on three sides by water, was a natural site for trade. With the influx of settlers from elsewhere in the colonies, as well as from Europe (French Huguenots, English, Irish, Scottish) and Barbados, Charles Towne grew to be the fifth-largest city in colonial America by 1690. A wealthy merchant class supported its bustling port.

To protect its citizens from attack by the Spanish and unfriendly Indians, fortified walls were built around the city in the late 17C along the boundaries of the Cooper River and present-day Meeting Street. By 1717, however, the walls were taken down to make room for the expanding city.

The End of the Lord Proprietors

When King Charles II returned from exile in 1661 to assume the English throne, he showed his gratitude to those who had been most loyal to him by naming eight Lord Proprietors and granting to them all the territory now occupied by North Carolina, South Carolina and Georgia.

The Lord Proprietors, however, took little interest in the colonies that were established on their lands. After their overseers failed to send troops to protect Charles Towne from Spanish attack, the colonists revolted. One thing led to another, and in 1721, the reign of the Lord Proprietors ended when South Carolina became a royal colony, under a British governor.

Rice, indigo and cotton thrived along the coast in the Lowcountry's temperate, humid climate, and soon hundreds of plantations—largely dependent on slave laborers brought from the west coast of Africa—dotted the landscape.

The Civil War, which heard its first shots in Charleston Harbor in the early morning hours of April 12, 1861, changed the city forever. By war's end, the once-thriving port had been shelled into a virtual ghost town. As a result of the abolition of slavery and the poverty that besieged the South after the war, the region's plantation economy gradually disintegrated.

Hounded by natural disasters over the years, plucky Charleston has rebuilt itself after repeated fires, hurricanes and earthquakes (the city sits on the second most active fault in the US). In order to protect its historic structures, Charleston became the first American city to enact a historic zoning ordinance in 1931, thus becoming a model for the preservation movement. Today Charleston is known for its stunning 18C and 19C **architecture**★★★.

In recent decades, the coast has spiffed itself up with even greater family appeal. Charleston opened the new South Carolina Aquarium on Aquarium Wharf *(see Musts for Kids)*, and Myrtle Beach has added new shopping centers, entertainment venues and amusement parks to its already impressive roster of attractions.

Like any gracious Southern lady, the South Carolina Coast always welcomes visitors. Any season is a good one to bask on the area's wide sandy beaches, revel in its historic architecture, and breathe its magnolia-scented air.

Fast Facts

- In 2004, for the twelfth consecutive year, Charleston was ranked among the Top 10 Travel Destinations in North America by *Condé Nast Traveler* magazine.

- Some 13 million people visit the Myrtle Beach area every year. They can choose accommodations among 72,400 units in hotels, motels and condominiums.

- Antebellum plantation owners turned Pawleys Island into one of the first summer resorts on the Atlantic Coast.

- Charleston boasts the fourth-largest container port in the US, handling more than 15 million tons of cargo a year.

Historic District

Any visit to Charleston should begin on the lower tip of the 5.2-square-mile peninsula formed by the Ashley and Cooper rivers. This is the **Historic District**★★★, heart of Charleston since 1680, which encompasses the area specified in the original 17C Grand Modell, or city plan. As you stroll the palmetto-studded streets lined with gas lanterns, it's easy to imagine the colonial days when Charleston was London in miniature—a prosperous aristocratic city whose gentry built many of the home you see today.

> **Touring Tip**
>
> If you like historic houses, you can save a few bucks by purchasing a combination ticket *($14)* for the Nathaniel Russell and Aiken-Rhett houses, both of which are operated by the Historic Charleston Foundation.

Here, you'll discover some of the city's most legendary sights and its loveliest structures, along with a multitude of boutiques, antique shops and restaurants that cater to a wide range of tastes and pocketbooks.

Nathaniel Russell House★★★

51 Meeting St. 843-724-8481. www.historiccharleston.org. Visit by 30-minute guided tour only, year-round Mon–Sat 10am–5pm, Sun 2pm–5pm. Closed Thanksgiving Day & Dec 24–25. $8. Combination tickets are available for Nathaniel Russell and Aiken-Rhett houses.

If you just see one historic house in Charleston, make it this one. Sister property to the Aiken-Rhett House *(p 25)*, the Nathaniel Russell House has been restored to its 19C glory after the roof collapsed when Hurricane Hugo blew through town in 1989. The Federal-style brick residence, considered to be one of the best examples of this architectural style in the US, was built in 1808 for

Nathaniel Russell and his wife, Sarah. Born in Rhode Island, Russell came to Charleston at age 27 in 1765, as an agent for a Providence import-export firm. When he moved his family into the new house in 1808, Russell was 70 years old, and ranked as one of the city's wealthiest merchants. You can see his prosperity for yourself in the ornate carved woodwork and moldings, and the collections of fine 18C Charleston-made antiques and English silver that decorate the lovely rooms.

Hey, Honey—Wanna Joggle?

The first thing the tour guide will point out to you at Nathaniel Russell House is the **joggling board**, which looks like a sort of garden seat. You might think it's a children's toy—and indeed, kids through the centuries have loved them—but in 19C Charleston, joggling boards were used more often by courting couples. It's said that a home that had a joggling board never had an unmarried daughter. Try it with a friend and see for yourself: as you bounce gently on the board, your partner will slip closer and closer.

To get one for your garden, contact the Old Charleston Joggling Board Company *(652 King St.; 843-723-4331; www.oldcharlestonjogglingboard.com)*.

What's Inside?

- The Nathaniel Russell House is famed for its **"flying" staircase**—a free-standing spiral that circles up, seemingly unsupported, to the third floor.

- Rooms are laid out in identical symmetrical suites—rectangular, oval and square—on each of the three floors.

- The lovely oval **Music Room** was used for entertaining Charleston's elite. Resembling windows, the room's large paneled mirrors were intended to reflect the firelight.

What's Outside?

- A formal English garden flanks the house with boxwood hedges and plants favored by 19C Charlestonians. An amateur gardener, Mrs. Russell first festooned this "urban plantation" with flowers, myrtle bowers, and lemon and orange trees.

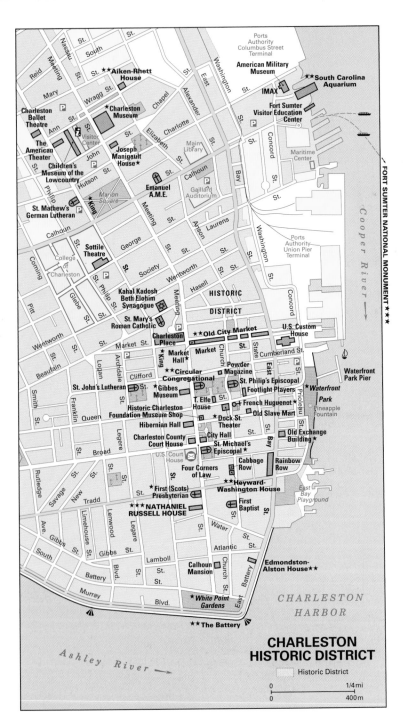

CHARLESTON
HISTORIC DISTRICT

Historic District

0   1/4 mi
0   400m

Aiken-Rhett House★★

48 Elizabeth St. 843-724-8481. www.historiccharleston.org. Visit by 30-minute guided tour only, year-round Mon–Sat 10am–5pm, Sun 2pm–5pm. Closed Thanksgiving Day & Dec 24–25. $8. Combination tickets are available for Aiken-Rhett and Nathaniel Russell houses.

What's the difference between conservation and restoration? The answer will be clear after you visit the Aiken-Rhett House and its sister property, the **Nathaniel Russell House**★★★ *(p 22)*, both of which are maintained by the Historic Charleston Foundation. Unlike other Charleston historic homes that have been restored to their former elegance, the Aiken-Rhett House has been preserved as it appeared c.1860.

Built as a Federal-style brick double house *(see sidebar below)* in 1817, the home was purchased in 1827 by wealthy cotton merchant William Aiken Sr. After his death, his son, William Jr., inherited the house with his wife, Harriet. The new owners made significant changes to the structure, moving the front entrance, building a large addition, and reconfiguring the first floor with an arched marble entry-hall staircase, gracious double parlors and an art gallery.

The Single House

As you wander through the historic district, you'll notice narrow houses where the porch faces the side instead of the street. This is a single house, Charleston's distinctive contribution to American architecture, which is based on a typical West Indian design (many of Charleston's early settlers were planters from Barbados). The typical single house is one room wide and two rooms deep, and includes a long piazza—the Charleston term for the airy porches designed to catch prevailing breezes—lying behind a "false" front door on the narrow side of the house that opens onto the street. The real entrance to the house is off the piazza. A variation on this theme, the **double house** is a near square with a room in each corner, divided by a central hall.

Aiken, who served as governor of South Carolina from 1844 to 1846, died in 1887, and Harriet converted the ballroom into her bedroom and closed off several rooms, furnishings and all. After her death, Harriet's daughter did little to maintain the house, except to add electricity to several rooms. When the Historic Charleston Foundation acquired the crumbling property in 1995, they opted to clean, stabilize and preserve it, just as they'd found it.

Interior – Today, the eerie ravages of time are evident in the rooms, especially in the occasional pieces of original furniture with their tattered fabric, and in the peeling wallpaper—but that's all part of the property's charm.

Grounds – Out back, the original 1817 outbuildings (typical of every 19C town house in Charleston) include the slaves' quarters, kitchen and stables.

The Battery★★

If you've seen any photographs of Charleston, chances are you've seen the Battery—it figures prominently on almost every advertisement for the city (and on every other souvenir you find in town). Indeed, this historic district landmark defines the tip of Charleston's peninsula.

Long considered a strategic point from which to defend the city, the Battery takes its nickname from its military service. The site is protected by a high seawall that lines the Cooper River side of Charleston Harbor; this wall replaced the masonry structure built in 1700 to fortify the city. Strengthened over the years to ward off hurricanes—including Hurricane Hugo in 1989—the wall became known as the High Battery for the gun emplacement stationed here during the War of 1812. Earthen batteries were constructed during the Civil War, although they never saw much action. After the war ended in 1865, the Battery reverted to more peaceful uses as a park.

What's Not To Like About The Battery?

Views★★★ – Walkers, joggers and hosts of visitors frequent the pretty oleander-lined promenade to savor **views★★★** of the river and of the graceful homes that line East and South Battery (depending on which side of the corner they're located).

Architecture★★★ – The elegant pastel mansions set along the Battery, positioned so that their airy piazzas catch the prevailing breezes off the river, provide stellar examples of Charleston's noted antebellum residential architecture.

White Point Gardens★ – *See Parks and Gardens*. At the seaside corner of East Bay Street, the lovely green space is named for the mounds of sun-bleached oyster shells that once accumulated here.

The Last Big One: Hurricane Hugo

On September 21, 1989, a category-four hurricane by the name of Hugo slammed into the South Carolina coast, boasting winds of up to 135mph and a storm surge of 20 feet—the highest tidal surge ever recorded in the state. Although the barrier islands suffered the brunt of the storm, in downtown Charleston 60 buildings were flattened, 5,100 homes were destroyed, and nearly 12,000 homes were left uninhabitable after the tempest passed. In addition to a death toll of 26 people in South Carolina, Hurricane Hugo racked up a whopping $7.2 billion worth of damage.

Edmondston-Alston House★★

21 East Battery. 843-722-7171. www.middletonplace.org. Visit by 30-minute guided tour only, year-round Tue–Sat 10am–4:30pm, Sun & Mon 1:30pm–4:30pm. Closed Thanksgiving Day & Dec 25. $10.

Imagine what tales this stunning house could tell, overlooking the harbor as it has since 1825, when it was built for Scotsman and cotton trader Charles Edmondston as the first house on the High Battery. When the cotton market turned sour 13 years later, Edmondston sold the property to moneyed Charleston rice planter Colonel William Alston,  whose son, Charles, lived in the house and added the third-floor piazza and other Greek Revival details, which were all the rage at the time.

A tour of the exquisitely decorated mansion, with its three airy piazzas supported by Doric and Corinthian columns, depicts the life of Charleston's 19C elite. Here you'll find Alston family furnishings, silver, and a collection of more than 1,000 rare volumes in Charles Alston's second-floor library.

21 East Battery Bed & Breakfast

21 East Battery. 843-556-0500 or 800-543-4664. www.21eastbattery.com. Rates range from $195–$350, depending on the season. You may not be able to spend the night in the Edmondston-Alston House, but you can stay on the grounds of this urban complex in Charles Edmonston's 1825 carriage house. Now a B&B, the inn offers guests a choice of three rooms with private baths. Rates include a gourmet breakfast and a complimentary tour of the Edmondston-Alston House.

Heyward-Washington House★★

87 Church St. 843-722-2996. www.charlestonmuseum.org. Visit by 30-minute guided tour only, year-round Mon–Sat 10am–5pm, Sun 1pm–5pm. Closed major holidays. $8. Combination tickets available for Heyward-Washington House, Joseph Manigault House and the Charleston Museum.

Named for its original owner, patriot Thomas Heyward, this redbrick double house is an oddity in Charleston; it remains structurally unchanged from 1772 when it was built within the boundaries of the old walled city. And yes, George Washington did sleep here during a visit to Charleston in 1791—thus the second part of the home's name.

Heyward distinguished himself as a signer of the Declaration of Independence, as a criminal court judge and as an officer in the South Carolina militia during the Revolution. When you tour his home, you'll get a first-hand glimpse at the luxuries a man of his status would have enjoyed in colonial Charleston.

Touring Tip

Heyward-Washington House, Joseph Manigault House *(p 32)* and the Charleston Museum *(see Museums)* are all operated by the museum. You can save a few dollars if you buy a combination ticket for two sites *($14)*, but your best deal is to buy a ticket for all three sites *($18)*—a savings of $7.

Thomas Elfe

Born in England, cabinetmaker Thomas Elfe emigrated to Charles Towne, as it was then called, in 1747 and established himself as a tradesman in the thriving city. His skill soon made him one of the most sought-after cabinetmakers in the area, and a relative millionaire in his day. Inspired by Thomas Chippendale, who was his contemporary, Elfe made more than 1,500 pieces between 1768 and his death in 1775, including beds, chairs, bookcases and desks.

In addition to visiting the Heyward-Washington House, you can see some of Elfe's pieces in the **Thomas Elfe House**, set up as it was when he lived there in the mid-18C *(54 Queen St.; 843-722-9161; visit by 30-minute guided tour only, year-round Mon–Fri 10am–noon; closed weekends & major holidays; $5).*

Outside, you can see the original kitchen, as well as the pretty formal garden, which contains symmetrical plots of camellias, tea olives, boxwood, roses and herbs—all plants introduced to the Lowcountry before 1791.

Furniture Collection★ – Inside, the rooms are decorated with a remarkable collection of 18C Charleston-made furniture, including the priceless Holmes bookcase—which survived British mortar fire during the Revolutionary War—as well as pieces attributed to skilled cabinetmaker Thomas Elfe *(see sidebar, p 29)*.

Old City Market★★

On Market St. between Meeting & E. Bay Sts.

A trip to Charleston just isn't complete without a stroll through the Old City Market. Stretching from Meeting Street to the river along Market Street, the three-block-long row of open-air sheds with arched openings fills daily with vendors selling everything from sweet grass baskets to T-shirts *(see Must Shop)*. The site where the stalls now stand used to be marshland belonging to the Pinckney family *(see Plantations)*, who donated it for use as a city market in the late 1700s. At the turn of the 19C, the swampy plot was filled in to create a meat and produce market. For years, the market served as the commercial hub of the city.

Old Slave Mart

6 Chalmers St. Closed for renovation.

Despite what you might have heard, the Old City Market was not the site of slave auctions in the years before Emancipation. That dubious distinction goes to the Old Slave Mart, located on cobblestone Chalmers Street. Slave marts like this one sprang up around the district beginning in 1856, when the practice of selling slaves on the side of the Custom House (now the Old Exchange Building; *see p 34*) was outlawed. The open-ended mart had just one large room inside, while the high arched entrance boasted grand octagonal pillars and a large iron gate.

Market Hall★ – *Market St. at Meeting St.* You'll know you're at the market when you see the elegant 1841 Greek Revival landmark that stands like a sentinel in front of the market sheds. Designed by local architect Edward Brickell White, Market Hall resembles a Roman temple. The structure was recently restored to its 19C grandeur—to the tune of $3.6 million—after sustaining severe damage during Hurri-

cane Hugo in 1989. Although Market Hall's exterior may look like stone, it's really made from brick covered with stucco scored to resemble stone blocks; the brownstone steps and trim take on a reddish hue in the sunlight. Notice the sheep and bull skulls on the stucco frieze; they refer back to the original 19C meat market that once stood on this spot.

Confederate Museum – Market Hall now houses a collection of Civil War memorabilia on its second floor *(see Museums)*.

Calhoun Mansion

16 Meeting St. Not open to the public. With 24,000 square feet of living space, Calhoun Mansion ranks as Charleston's largest single residence. Built in 1876 for wealthy banker George Williams, the home passed to Williams' daughter Sally and her husband, Patrick Calhoun (grandson of statesman John C. Calhoun). The mansion encompasses 35 rooms; the airy second-floor music room rises 45 feet high to a glass skylight. Once open to the public for tours, the mansion was recently sold and is now a private residence.

Dock Street Theatre★

135 Church St., at Queen St.
843-577-5967 or 800-454-7093.
www.charlestonstage.com.

You'll recognize this Church Street fixture by its lacy wrought-iron balcony, which looks like something you'd see in New Orlean's French Quarter. Constructed as a hotel in 1809, the building now provides performance space for the Charleston Stage Company. Renovated as part of a WPA project in the 1930s, the theater claims to be the first building in America designed specifically for theatrical performances *(for performance and ticket information, see Performing Arts).*

Four Corners of Law

Originally intended to be a grand public square, the four corners of the intersection of Broad and Meeting streets hold public buildings that each represents a different branch of the law:

• Completed in 1788, the **Charleston County Court House**, on the northwest corner, exemplifies state law.

• The 1896 Renaissance Revival **U.S. Court House and Post Office**, on the southwest corner, represents federal law.

• On the northeast corner, Palladian-style **City Hall**, built in 1801, stands in for municipal law.

• **St. Michael's Episcopal Church★**, which graces the southeast corner, represents God's law *(see Historic Sites).*

Joseph Manigault House★

350 Meeting St., at the corner of John St.
843-722-2996. www.charlestonmuseum.org.
Visit by 30-minute guided tour only, year-round Mon–Sat 10am–5pm, Sun 1pm–5pm.
Closed major holidays. $8. Combination tickets are available for Heyward-Washington House, Joseph Manigault House and the Charleston Museum.

Gentleman-architect Gabriel Manigault designed this graceful three-story brick residence, with its distinctive half-moon-shaped piazza *(north side),* for his brother Joseph in 1803.

Located just across from Charleston Museum (and the Visitor Reception Center), the house captures the lifestyle of prosperous early-19C Huguenot rice planters. Typical of the Adam (or Federal) style of architecture—named for English architect Robert Adam—the house incorporates a variety of shapes, such as arched doorways, a sinuous staircase, and fanlights. Throughout the residence, you'll see delicately carved woodwork, another earmark of the Adam style, as well as a group of French, English and American 19C furniture from the Charleston Museum's fine collection.

Preserving the Past

Ravaged by the Civil War and the ensuing years of Reconstruction, Charleston by the 1920s was a shadow of its former self. With its economy faltering, the city had no money to fix up its grand colonial and antebellum houses, many of which were literally crumbling with age and neglect. Charlestonians at the time were, as they put it, "too poor to paint, too proud to whitewash."

Spurred partly by the cultural re-awakening of the Charleston Renaissance *(see p 78)*, Charleston in 1931 became the first city in America to enact a major preservation ordinance to save its historic treasures. Thanks to the efforts of the Historic Charleston Foundation, founded in 1947 to "preserve and protect the integrity of Charleston's architectural, historical and cultural heritage," and other preservation organizations, Charleston's restored antebellum residential **architecture**★★★ today ranks among the best in the country.

Stop in at the **Historic Charleston Foundation Museum Shop** *(108 Meeting St. See Must Shop)*, where you can pick up a copy of the Historic District walking-tour booklet. There's also a good display here explaining the mix of architectural styles you'll find in Charleston.

Old Exchange Building★

122 E. Bay St., at Broad St. 843-727-2165. www.oldexchange.com. Open year-round daily 9am–5pm. Closed Jan 1, Thanksgiving Day & Dec 25. $7.

The Old Exchange Building is remarkable in several ways. Constructed in 1771 on the site of Half-Moon Bastion—part of the original fortifications around the city—the Georgian-style Exchange and Custom House with its arched Palladian windows was the last structure that the British erected in Charleston. It's one of only three buildings in the country where the US Constitution was ratified in 1788 (the other two were Independence Hall in Philadelphia and Faneuil Hall in Boston). Some of the very men who signed the document had been imprisoned downstairs in the damp, gloomy Provost Dungeon during the British occupation of the city. Displays inside detail the building's history, especially its connection to America's fight for independence.

Provost Dungeon – *Visit by 20-minute guided tour only.* Kids will enjoy the tour of the spooky dungeon, now outfitted with animatronic figures representing characters from the city's past, who tell their tales to any willing audience. This is the one place in town where you can see part of the **original seawall** built in the late 17C to fortify the city.

The Charleston Tea Party

Sure, you've heard of the Boston Tea Party, but did you know there was a similar incident in Charleston? There was no dumping of tea into the harbor here, but Patriots did attempt to seize a shipment of 256 chests of East India Company tea from Britain. They were protesting the fact that the British government authorized the company to export tea without paying the usual customs duties, thus giving them an unfair advantage over colonial merchants. After meeting with the colonists, representatives of the East India Company agreed not to accept shipment of the tea, and customs officials took possession of the goods for non-payment of duties. The chests were stored in the Exchange warehouse until the Revolution broke out in 1776, at which time the confiscated tea was sold to raise money for the colonial army. How's that for an ironic twist?

The Rest of the Historic District's Best

Hibernian Hall

105 Meeting St. Not open to the public.

Built in 1840, this National Historic Landmark was—and still is—the meeting place for the Ancient Order of Hibernians, an Irish Catholic organization whose members are devoted to the welfare of their fellow Irishmen. Hibernian Hall's claim to historical fame is the fact that it hosted the National Democratic Convention of 1860 for the party faction supporting Stephen A. Douglas to run against Abraham Lincoln (and we all know who won that vote).

The hall is pure Greek Revival in style, designed by Philadelphia architect Thomas U. Walter, whose work includes an expansion of the Capitol in Washington, DC. Notice the harp carved above the main door and incorporated into the iron entrance gate; this motif echoes the Irish heritage of the hall's founders.

Powder Magazine

79 Cumberland St. 843-722-3767. Open year-round Mon–Sat 10am–5pm, Sun 2pm–5pm.

Understandably, there are few structures that survive today from the days when Charleston was the domain of the Lord Proprietors appointed by King Charles II. The windowless, tile-roof Powder Magazine, completed in 1713, is one of them. Inside its 32-inch-thick walls, soldiers stored munitions and gunpowder used to defend the fortified city against attack from Spanish

troops, hostile Indians and marauding pirates. (The cannons out front aren't quite that old, though; they date from the Revolutionary War.) It's worth a walk through the oldest public building in the city, where an interactive exhibit tells the story of Charleston's earliest days.

U.S. Custom House

200 E. Bay St. Not open to the public.

The stately white United States Custom House lords it over East Bay Street at the foot of Market Street. Shaped in a cross, the monumental structure measures 259 feet on its east-west axis and 152 feet on its north-south axis. Construction began in 1853, but engineering problems, lack of funding, and damage caused by the intervening Civil War delayed its completion until 1879. Ever since then, it has operated as a US Customs facility.

Keeper of the Gates

As you explore the historic district, be sure to notice the wrought- and cast-ironwork that adorns many of the garden gates. Charleston rivals New Orleans in this decorative art form, which evolved from 19C plantation blacksmiths who made and repaired tools. Today, the best examples of this art are fashioned by Charleston's favorite son, Philip Simmons, known world-wide for his decorative ironwork. Born on nearby Daniel Island in 1912, Simmons' work appears in some 500 gates, balconies and fences throughout the district. In 1982 Simmons was named a National Folk Treasure by the Smithsonian and the National Park Service when one of his gates was displayed at the Smithsonian Institution's National Museum of American History in Washington, DC. Now 92 years old, Simmons still practices his art in Charleston. For more on Simmons' designs, check online at: *www.philipsimmons.org*.

Rows of Row Houses

Rainbow Row – *79-107 E. Bay St.* A favorite Charleston photo subject, the bright multicolored row of colonial town houses reigns as the largest intact cluster of Georgian row houses in the US. The earliest of these dwellings, which were built as merchants' residences, dates to 1740.

Cabbage Row – *89-91 Church St.* In the 1920s, poor black residents of this late-18C double tenement used to sell vegetables from their windowsills, thus giving the site its nickname. These residences provided the inspiration for "Catfish Row" in Dubose Heyward's 1925 novel, *Porgy*. Heyward's story became the basis for George Gershwin's folk opera *Porgy and Bess*, a fictional look at black life in 1920s Charleston. Today the dwellings are filled with shops.

✳

Since its founding in 1670, Charleston has known some pretty momentous events. The first great victory of the Revolution was won here at Fort Moultrie in 1776, and the first shots of the Civil War were fired in Charleston Harbor in 1861. More recently, in 2000, the Civil War-era submarine *H.L. Hunley* was raised from the depths of the harbor. But don't just read about it—come discover Charleston's fascinating history for yourself.

Fort Sumter National Monument★★★

Accessible only by boat from Patriots Point or the Fort Sumter Visitor Education Center, located on Liberty Square (next to the aquarium at the east end of Calhoun St.). 843-577-0242. www.nps.gov/fosu. Open Apr–Labor Day 10am–5:30pm; rest of the year, call for hours. Closed Jan 1, Thanksgiving Day & Dec 25. Fee for cruise includes admission to fort (see sidebar below).

Getting to the Fort

As an authorized concessionaire of the National Park Service, SpiritLine Cruises offers the only commercial boat transportation to Fort Sumter. Boats depart from the **Fort Sumter Visitor Education Center** on Liberty Square *(opposite)*, and from **Patriots Point Naval Maritime Museum★★** in Mt. Pleasant *(see Musts for Kids)*. During the 30-minute narrated cruise, you'll learn about some of the events leading up to the war. *Allow 2 hours to visit the fort, including the boat trip. For boat schedules, call 843-881-7337. www.fortsumtertours.com. $12 adults, $6 children (children under age 6 ride free).*

Imagine this lonely outpost at the entrance to Charleston Harbor alive with cannon fire, men running and shouting, the powder magazines exploding in flames. This was the scene on April 12, 1861, when Confederate forces fired the first shots of the Civil War.

When South Carolina seceded from the Union on December 20, 1860, four forts guarded the entrance to Charleston Harbor: Fort Sumter on its manmade island, Fort Moultrie on Sullivans Island *(see p 40)*, Fort Johnson on James Island, and Castle Pinckney on Shutes Folly Island. The five-sided brick fort, named for South Carolina Revolutionary War hero Thomas Sumter, was 90 percent complete at the time, but only 15 of the fort's more than 100 cannons stood mounted and ready.

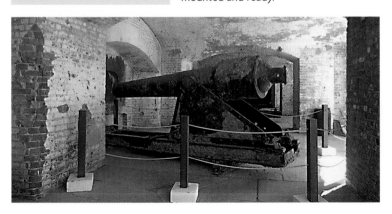

On December 26, Union major Robert Anderson secretly relocated his cadre of 85 men from Fort Moultrie to Fort Sumter—a move that South Carolina responded to by demanding the evacuation of Charleston Harbor by U.S. Government forces. Over the ensuing months, government attempts to resupply the fort led to increasing tensions between the North and South.

Fort Facts

- It took seven million bricks to build Fort Sumter.
- Outer walls were five feet thick.
- The fort's three tiers rose 50 feet above water level.
- Designed for a garrison of 650 men, the fort could bear an armament of 135 guns.

A final try at getting supplies through to Sumter in April 1861 pushed General P.G.T. Beauregard, commander of the Confederate troops in Charleston, to ask Major Anderson to surrender the stronghold. When Anderson refused, Confederate officers informed him that their forces would open fire in an hour. At 3:30am on April 12, 1861, Rebels fired on Sumter. The cannonade continued for 34 hours, until Major Anderson finally surrendered the fort on April 13.

"The firing of the mortar woke the echoes from every nook and corner of the harbour . . . ," wrote Stephen Lee, aide-de-camp to General Beauregard, who commanded the Confederate forces. "A thrill went through the whole city. It was felt that the Rubicon was passed . . ."

After the Civil War ended in 1865, Fort Sumter stood neglected until 1898, when it was used during the Spanish-American War. The fort was decommissioned in 1947 and transferred to the National Park Service the following year.

Visiting Fort Sumter

Fort Sumter Visitor Education Center – *Next to the aquarium at the east end of Calhoun St.* This is the place to begin and to purchase tickets for the boat trip to the fort. Displays detail the events leading up to the first shots of the Civil War. Artifacts here include Major Anderson's original garrison flag that waved over Fort Sumter.

Fort Walking Tour – Once at the fort, you can inspect the casemates and the ruins of the barracks and officers' quarters on the self-guided walking tour. A **museum** in Battery Huger, added in 1899, tells the story of the fort and its role in the Civil War through informative panels, armaments and artifacts.

Fort Moultrie★

1214 Middle St., on Sullivans Island. 9mi northeast of Charleston via US-17 North & Rte. 703. 843-883-3123. www.nps.gov/fomo. Open year-round 9am–5pm. Closed Jan 1, Thanksgiving Day & Dec 25. $3 (free for children 16 and under).

What's in a fort? In this case, wood and sand. Hastily built with wood from abundant local palmetto trees, the first fort on Sullivans Island was constructed in 1776 to protect Charleston from British attack. Soon after, Fort Moultrie gained fame as the crude rampart that held off the British during the battle for Sullivans Island. Soft palmetto logs that formed the walls of the early fort helped thwart the Redcoats' attack by absorbing the British shells. After the battle, the palmetto tree was adopted as the South Carolina state symbol.

In 1794 Fort Moultrie was rebuilt as a five-sided battlement with earth and timber walls; this version was destroyed by a hurricane in 1804. The third incarnation of the fort—and the one you see here now—arose in 1809, and saw action through World War II. Fort Moultrie was decommissioned in 1947, the same year as Fort Sumter.

Palmetto Flag, Palmetto State

Why is South Carolina's state flag decorated with a palmetto tree? The answer to that question makes a good story. The design derives from the one that graced the flag carried by South Carolina's Palmetto Guard. Members of the unit planted this standard on Fort Sumter's parapet in April 1861, when Confederate troops took Fort Sumter. Adopted in January 1861, the South Carolina State flag bears a palmetto tree in honor of the soft palmetto logs that saved Fort Moultrie from British attack in 1776. Ever since 1861, South Carolina has been known as the Palmetto State.

As you walk through the fort today, you'll find remainders from every period of its long history:

- The site of the first fort
- Cannon Walk, with its Civil War artillery
- Two batteries that defended the harbor from 1898
- World War II Control Post

Outside the fort's Sally Port lie the graves of the Seminole leader Osceola, who died here in 1838, and 5 of the 62 crewman who died when the US warship *Patapsco* was sunk in nearby waters in 1965.

Charles Towne Landing State Historic Site

1500 Old Towne Rd., 3mi northwest of Charleston via US-17 to Rte. 171. 843-852-4200. www.southcarolinaparks.com. Open Memorial Day–Labor Day daily 8:30am–6pm. Rest of the year daily 8:30am–5pm. Closed Dec 24 & 25. $5 adults, $3 children (ages 6-15).

History comes alive at Charles Towne Landing, on the very spot where the first English colonists landed in 1670. Here, they built a fort on Old Towne Creek and planted the fields with wheat, oranges, tobacco and other crops. Named Charles Towne, for King Charles II of England, the settlement only lasted ten years in these swampy, mosquito-infested lands along the river. Plagued by disease and hunger, the colonists moved the town site across the river to the Charleston peninsula in 1680.

Experience early colonial life and explore the ruins of the first settlement, including a reconstruction of the original palisade wall. You'll see archaeology in action here, as scientists constantly uncover the site's hidden past.

Trails and Gardens – Seven miles of trails for hiking and biking lace the site. Also here are 80 acres of gardens, including an Experimental Crop Garden showcasing some of the crops—indigo, rice, sugarcane, cotton—the settlers tried to grow here.

Animal Forest – See the creatures the settlers met here. *See Musts for Kids.*

The Adventure – Although this full-size replica of a 17C trading vessel is currently closed to the public, you can watch the restoration efforts; the ship is in dry dock right next to the river. The *Adventure* is scheduled to be open for tours again later in 2005.

Legare-Waring House – The former summer residence of South Carolina's governors is open only as a special-events venue.

Fickle Finger of Fate

Known as the Merry Monarch, King Charles II returned from exile in 1661 to assume his rightful throne. To reward those who had been most loyal to him, the King granted all the territory now occupied by North Carolina, South Carolina and Georgia to eight Lord Proprietors.

In an interesting bit of historic irony, the Ashley and Cooper rivers in Charleston are named for one of the Lord Proprietors, Anthony Ashley Cooper, Earl of Shaftesbury, who was later imprisoned for plotting against his benefactor, King Charles.

The Citadel

171 Moultrie St. 843-953-6779. www.citadel.edu. Campus is open to visitors daily 8am–6pm.

Rising northwest of the historic district along the Ashley River, the white Moorish-style notched walls of the Citadel buildings surround green Summerall Field. This well-known military academy began in 1829 as an arsenal and guardhouse to protect the city of Charleston. At that time, the Citadel was located on Marion Square *(Calhoun & Meeting Sts.)* in what is now "downtown" Charleston (the original building, now painted pink, remains on the square as an Embassy Suites hotel). In 1842 the Citadel, along with the Arsenal in Columbia, South Carolina, was converted into the South Carolina Military Academy. The academy remained on Marion Square until 1910, when it acquired the 200-acre campus on which it's now located.

Touring the Campus – Cadet-led tours of the campus are available during the school year *(to arrange a guided tour, call 843-953-6779)*. If you want to explore on your own, you can pick up a walking-tour brochure at the museum, and hit the major points of interest. In addition to those sites listed below, several monuments on the grounds honor the heroism of Citadel graduates.

- Gothic-style **Summerall Chapel** is a popular venue for cadet weddings.

- **Mark Clark Grave** is the burial place of General Mark W. Clark, former president of the Citadel and one of the top five American military commanders of World War II.

- The 90-foot-high **Thomas Dry Howie Carillon Tower** rings out concerts with its 59 Dutch bells.

- Inside Daniel Library, the **Citadel Murals** illustrate the academy's history.

Military Dress Parade

If you're into pomp and circumstance, come on Friday afternoon at 3:45pm during the college year to see the cadets march across central Summerall Field in their crisp full-dress uniforms. Afterwards, you can stop by the Citadel gift shop and pick up a souvenir.

The Citadel Museum – *Just inside the Lesesne Gate on the right (access via Moultrie St.). Third floor. 843-953-6846. www.citadel.edu/archivesandmuseum. Open year-round Sun–Fri 2pm–5pm, Sat noon–5pm. Closed for college & major holidays.* Come see what it's like to be a cadet at the Military College of South Carolina. Inside this small museum, historic photos, uniforms, weapons, medals and other artifacts tell the story of the Citadel, from its founding in 1842 to its involvement in contemporary military operations around the world.

The H.L. Hunley

Located on Charleston's former Naval Base. From I-26, take Exit 216B/Cosgrove Ave. North. 843-744-2186. www.hunley.org. Visit by 30-minute guided tour only, year-round Sat 10am–5pm & Sun noon–5pm. Closed holiday weekends. $10 (free for children under age 5).

Off the coast of Charleston on the night of February 17, 1864, the Confederate submarine *H.L. Hunley* fired a 135-pound torpedo into the Union Navy warship USS *Housatonic*, successfully sinking it. The crew on this cylindrical iron boiler, held together with strips of iron and rivets, signaled to shore that they had completed their mission and were on their way back. Then, mysteriously, the sub disappeared.

Touring Tip

Reservations are not required for the *Hunley* tours, but you can buy tickets in advance by calling 877-448-6539 or online at www.etix.com.

In 1995, after being lost at sea for 131 years, the *Hunley* was found buried in the ocean floor just outside Charleston Harbor by adventurer Clive Cussler. The raising of the *Hunley*, a joint undertaking of the Department of the Navy, the Park Service, Oceaneering International Inc., and Friends of the Hunley, was a feat of oceanic proportions. From a platform composed of two massive suction piles (the type used for mooring deepwater oil rigs) engineers lowered a truss onto the sub and positioned nylon slings with inflated foam pillows underneath the craft. On August 8, 2000, a crane lifted the entire truss to the surface and the *Hunley* was placed on a transport barge. Today a group of scientists in the Warren Lasch Conservation Center in North Charleston are slowly unraveling the mysteries of the *Hunley* and its courageous crew. You can view the sub in its conservation tank by taking one of the weekend tours.

End of a Journey

The eight-man crew who served aboard the *Hunley* were finally laid to rest on April 17, 2004. Ceremonies began in the morning with a poignant memorial service at White Point Garden. After the service, a procession led by horse-drawn caissons traveled through the historic district to Magnolia Cemetery on Charleston Neck *(70 Cunningham Ave.),* where 2,200 veterans of the Civil War are interred. Here, the crew of the *Hunley* was buried in front of a crowd of thousands of well-wishers, some of whom came from as far away as Australia.

If you're interested in visiting the cemetery at night, each October the Confederate Heritage Trust conducts its Ghost Walk by lantern light *(not recommended for young children). For information and tickets: 843-747-7554 or www.csatrust.org/ ghostwalk.htm.*

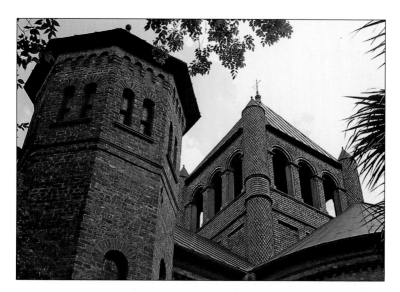

Historic Churches

Unlike Boston and Philadelphia, which were founded by Puritans and Quakers respectively, Charleston wasn't settled by any one religious group. Although the Anglican Church of England was predominant in the early city, Charleston promoted religious tolerance and the young city soon provided places of worship for many different beliefs. The spires of myriad churches are still visible across the peninsula today, giving rise to Charleston's nickname, "The Holy City."

Here's a selection of some of the most historic among the peninsula's 180 churches:

Fun Fact

Known as the White Meeting House, the white brick first Independent Church gave Meeting Street its name.

Circular Congregational Church★★ – *150 Meeting St.* Designed by Robert Mills, this striking brick Romanesque Revival church stands on the site of the first Independent Church, or Church for Dissenters (non-Anglicans), founded in 1681. The first circular church was built here in 1806; it burned in 1861 and its ruins fell during the 1886 earthquake. The graveyard you see now, the city's oldest, dates to 1695.

First (Scots) Presbyterian Church★ – *53 Meeting St.* You'll recognize the 1814 stucco-covered First Presbyterian Church by its columned Greek Revival facade and by the twin rounded towers that top its roof. This congregation was formed in 1731, when 12 Scottish families left the Independent Church and started their own meeting house, the "Scots Kirk." Out front, the wrought-iron gates incorporate a motif of thistles, the symbol of Scotland.

French Huguenot Church★ – *136 Church St.* Seeking to escape religious persecution in France, French Protestants, called Huguenots, came to Charleston beginning in the late 17C. The first church they built here was destroyed by fire in 1796. The graceful 1845 church, the third built on this site, was the first Gothic Revival structure in the city; its original pipe organ still provides music during services.

St. Michael's Episcopal Church★ –
80 Meeting St. George Washington might not have slept here, but he did worship in this 1761 Colonial-style church. Representing divine law on the intersection known as the **Four Corners of Law** *(see p 32)*, St. Michael's sits on the site of Charleston's original Anglican Church. Its 186-foot-high steeple was used as a lookout tower during the Revolution, and as a signal tower during the Civil War.

Emanuel A.M.E. Church – *110 Calhoun St.* The oldest Black congregation south of Baltimore, Maryland, attends services at Emanuel African Methodist Episcopal Church. Built in 1891, the Gothic-style church boasts a Victorian interior that retains its original altar, pews and light fixtures.

First Baptist Church – *61 Church St.* Designed by Charleston architect Robert Mills, the 1822 First Baptist Church reigns as the oldest Baptist church in the South. The original congregation was organized in Maine in 1692.

Kahal Kadosh Beth Elohim Synagogue – *90 Hassell St.* Built in 1840, this impressive Classical Revival-style National Historic Landmark is the second-oldest synagogue in the US, and the oldest one that's still in use. The American Reform Judaism Movement was born here in 1842.

> **Fun Fact**
>
> The tallest spire—297 feet—in Charleston belongs to **St. Mathew's German Lutheran Church** *(405 King St.).*

St. John's Lutheran Church – *5 Clifford St.* Charleston's oldest Lutheran congregation dates to 1742, but their first church wasn't completed until 1818. Added in 1859, the steeple with its bell-shaped top may have been the design of Charles Fraser, a Charleston architect and painter of miniatures.

St. Mary's Roman Catholic Church – *89 Hassell St.* Organized in 1788, the first Roman Catholic church in the Carolinas and Georgia had a large French congregation; if you walk through the churchyard, you'll notice that many of the gravestones are in French. The present Classical Revival church building was completed in 1839 to replace a brick building that burned down the previous year.

St. Philip's Episcopal Church – *146 Church St.* Organized in 1680, St. Philip's was founded the year the colonists moved to the peninsula from swampy Charles Towne. The present church dates to 1838; its lofty eight-sided steeple once held a light that guided sailors to Charleston's port.

> **St. Philip's Churchyard**
>
> The two sections of St. Philip's churchyard (east and west) hold the graves of some of the city's most prominent citizens and historical figures, including infamous South Carolina statesman and secessionist John C. Calhoun, and Edward Rutledge, a signer of the Declaration of Independence.

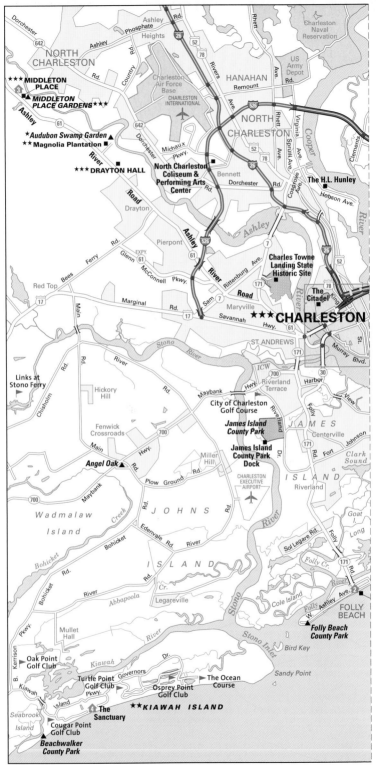

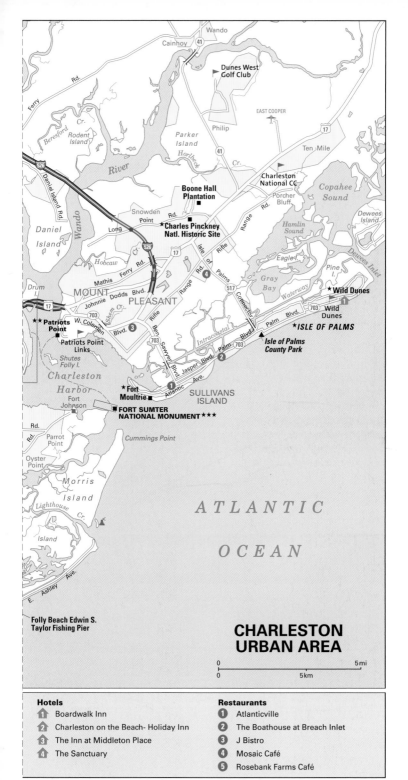

**CHARLESTON
URBAN AREA**

0   5mi
0   5km

Hotels

1. Boardwalk Inn
2. Charleston on the Beach- Holiday Inn
3. The Inn at Middleton Place
4. The Sanctuary

Restaurants

1. Atlanticville
2. The Boathouse at Breach Inlet
3. J Bistro
4. Mosaic Café
5. Rosebank Farms Café

Plantations

Shades of Rhett and Scarlett. Charleston's plantations hearken back to an era when rice flourished in flooded land along the rivers, providing riches for plantation owners and exhausting work for their slaves. Meandering up the south side of the Charleston peninsula, the Ashley River served in colonial times as the main route to the stately plantations that lined its banks. By land, an arduous back road traced part of an ancient Cherokee Indian trail. Today, tree-lined **Ashley River Road** (Route 61) provides easy access to all but a couple (two lie north of the city in Mt. Pleasant) of Charleston's plantations.

Drayton Hall★★★

3380 Ashley River Rd. 843-769-2600. www.draytonhall.org. Visit by 1-hour guided tour only, Mar–Oct daily 9:30am–4pm. Rest of the year daily 9:30am–3pm. Closed Jan 1 and Dec 24, 25 & 31. $12.

Considered to be one of the finest existing examples of Georgian-Palladian architecture in America, Drayton Hall is the only plantation house on the Ashley River to survive the Revolutionary and Civil wars intact. Completed in 1742 for John Drayton, the majestic brick mansion—whose architect is unknown—overlooks the river from its 630-acre site. Symmetry and classical detail distinguish the interior, which remains in nearly original condition.

How Did Drayton Hall Survive the Civil War?

No one seems to know for sure, but the story goes that in order to keep Union troops from occupying or destroying the mansion, the slaves who remained in the house put up yellow flags to indicate an outbreak of deadly yellow fever on the premises.

The Drayton family was literally divided during the Civil War, with one son fighting for the Union Army and the rest with the Confederate forces. Another theory holds that perhaps the son on the Union side used his influence to convince Yankee officers to spare his home.

Like their relatives at neighboring Magnolia Plantation, the Draytons weathered the poverty of the Reconstruction years by mining phosphate (used for fertilizer) on their land.

Royal Judge John Drayton used his country home from September to May for lavish entertaining and as a base from which to manage his many other estates. At his death, Drayton ranked as one of the wealthiest men in Carolina colony. The mansion was occupied by seven generations of the Drayton family before 1969, when it passed into the hands of the National Trust for Historic Preservation, which operates the site today.

Hall Highlights

Inside, you'll find no furnishings—those were sold at auction long ago—but you will see a wealth of ornate hand-carved and cast-plaster ceilings and hand-carved decorative moldings. The last finished coat of paint on the walls dates to 1885.

- Note that the grand **entrance** to Drayton Hall faced the river, since this was how most 18C and 19C guests arrived.

- The downstairs **Drawing Room** boasts a gorgeous ornate ceiling that was hand-molded in wet plaster.

- The Draytons used the upstairs **hall** for formal dining, dances and other social events. Doors here open onto the second story of the portico.

To the Manor Born: The Drayton Family

Descended from Norman aristocracy, ancestors of the modern-day Drayton family made their way to England via Aubrey de Vere, who came with William the Conqueror in 1066. After distinguishing himself during the Battle of Hastings, de Vere was awarded a Saxon castle in Northampton, known as Drayton House (de Vere later took the name of this property).

The first Draytons to come to America—Thomas and his son, Thomas Jr. *(see Magnolia Plantation)*—began a long line of that family in the mid-1600s, many of whom became prominent figures in American politics. John Drayton, who built Drayton Hall, was born next door at Magnolia Plantation in 1715.

A Muster of Middletons

The Middleton family exerted their fair share of influence in American politics over the generations:

Henry Middleton (1717–1784) – By the time of the Revolution, Henry owned 50,000 acres of land and 800 slaves. He was elected president of the First Continental Congress in 1774.

Arthur Middleton (1743–1787) – The eldest of Henry's five sons was one of the signers of the Declaration of Independence in 1776.

Henry Middleton (1770–1846) – Henry's grandson and Arthur's eldest son served as governor of South Carolina from 1810 to 1812 and as Ambassador to Russia during the 1820s.

Williams Middleton (1809–1883) – Henry's great-grandson (son of the second Henry) signed the Ordinance of Secession. His staunch support of the Confederate cause spurred Union troops to destroy his family's home in 1865.

Middleton Place★★★

4300 Ashley River Rd. 843-556-6020. www.middletonplace.org. Open year-round daily 9am–5pm. Closed Thanksgiving Day & Dec 25. General admission (gardens & grounds) $20 adults, $5 children (free for children under age 6). Combination tickets available for gardens, carriage ride and house tour: $39 adults, $28 children.

The land that came to Englishman Henry Middleton as part of his wife's dowry in 1741 now sweeps down to the Ashley River in 110 acres of green terraced lawns and symmetrical 18C English gardens. Laid out in 1741 by Henry Middleton, the gardens once formed part of the Middleton rice plantation.

Where Do I Begin?

If all this seems like too much to see in one day, make reservations at the Inn at Middleton Place *(see Must Stay)*. Even the little ones will like it here *(see Musts for Kids)*.

Gardens★★★ – The formal 18C English gardens burst into their fullest glory in early spring, but they're worth a visit at any time of year *(see Parks and Gardens)*.

House Museum – *Visit by 30-minute guided tour only, Tue–Sun 10am–4:30pm, Mon 1:30pm–4:30pm. $10 (in addition to general admission)*. Built as a gentleman's guest quarters in 1755, this brick dwelling is all that survives of the grand three-building complex that the Middleton family called home. The parts of the complex that weren't destroyed by the Union Army in 1865 toppled in the 1886 earthquake. Inside you'll find a fine collection of family furnishings and memorabilia.

Stableyards – Be sure to visit the stableyards to see what went on behind the scenes on a working colonial plantation. You'll find a flock of farm animals here, as well as artisans who demonstrate such essential skills as weaving, carpentry and blacksmithing.

Middleton Place Restaurant

Open for lunch daily, 11am–3pm. When you're ready for a break, treat yourself to lunch at airy Middleton Place Restaurant. Classic Southern fare rules the day here; many of the dishes have their origins in colonial times. Starters like peanut soup and okra gumbo both come from recipes brought to the area by African slaves. Entrées range from Southern fried chicken to barbecue pork. With your meal, you have your choice of sides that have a long history in the Lowcountry: Carolina Gold rice *(see p. 60)*, Hoppin' John, stone-ground grits, or sweet-potato casserole. All this and a garden view, too—how's that for local color?

Magnolia Plantation★★

3550 Ashley River Rd., west of Drayton Hall. 843-571-1266. www.magnoliaplantation.com. Open Mar–Oct daily 8am–5:30pm. Rest of the year daily 8am–5pm. $13 adults, $7 children (ages 6-12).

Touring Tip

If you don't have time to see all parts of the plantation in one visit, you can get a "rain check," which enables you to return free-of-charge on one other day within a seven-day period. You might want to pack a lunch when you come and dine alfresco in one of the lovely picnic areas on the grounds.

Home to 13 generations of the Drayton family, Magnolia Plantation has been open to the public since shortly after the Civil War, and is still owned by the family that created it. Magnolia's story begins in the mid-1600s, when an Englishman named Stephen Fox left Barbados for Charleston, where he acquired a 500-acre tract of land on the Ashley River (later named Magnolia Plantation). About the same time, Thomas Drayton, another wealthy Barbadian, came to town with his son, Thomas Jr. As it happened, Thomas Jr. ended up marrying Stephen Fox's daughter, Ann, who came with the plantation site as her dowry. Thomas built the original house at Magnolia Plantation, and the Drayton family has operated the estate ever since.

In 1820 the estate came into the hands of 22-year-old John Grimke Drayton, who later became a minister. Rev. Drayton developed the striking informal gardens here, to comfort his wife, Julia, who was homesick for her native city of Philadelphia.

Gardens – In bloom year-round, Magnolia's 50 acres of gardens are especially stunning in the springtime, when banks of bright azaleas color the grounds. *See Parks and Gardens.*

Plantation House – *Visit by 30-minute guided tour only. $7.* Completed in 1760, the Victoria manor that sits here today is the third dwelling on this site. The first two structures fell victim to fire (the second one was torched by General Sherman's men during the Civil War). After the war, the home you see here today was dismantled and floated down the Ashley River by barge from nearby Summerville. Tour guides highlight early plantation life and point out the many Drayton family heirlooms and the fine collection of early-American antiques that fill the rooms.

Audubon Swamp Garden★ – Opened in the 1980s, this 60-acre cypress and tupelo swamp is the most recent addition to the site *(see Parks and Gardens).*

All Aboard!

You could get pretty tired walking around all 500 acres of Magnolia Plantation, which has been managed as a wildlife refuge since 1975. Luckily, there are two other modes of transportation available at Magnolia: the **nature train**, which covers 4 miles of wildlife habitat on the plantation's outskirts; and the electric-powered **nature boat**, which cruises silently along canals that cut through a former rice field. Both offer 45-minute tours ($7) that are great for spotting wildlife, especially birds. Green-winged teals, red-tailed hawks, Eastern bluebirds and yellow-bellied sapsuckers number among the more than 200 species of birds you might see along the way.

Charles Pinckney National Historic Site★

1254 Long Point Rd., Mt. Pleasant, 7mi north of Charleston. Take US-17 North and turn left on Long Point Rd.; the historic site is across the street from Boone Hall. 843-881-5516. www.nps.gov/chpi. Open year-round daily 9am–5pm. Closed Jan 1, Thanksgiving Day & Dec 25.

Touring Tip

If you're on a budget, note that Snee Farm is the only Charleston area plantation where admission to both the house and grounds is free. Take a few minutes (20, to be exact) to watch the informative video, shown in the cottage, that details the history of Snee Farm and its owner, Charles Pinckney.

Patriot and planter Charles Pinckney inherited this Lowcountry estate from his father in 1782. Dubbed Snee Farm, the plantation was Pinckney's favorite "country seat," among the many properties owned by his influential family. Pinckney, who spent much time away from the plantation seeing to affairs of state, was forced to sell the farm in 1817 to settle his debts. Today only 28 of the property's original 715 acres remain undeveloped.

Although no structures are left from the time when the Pinckneys lived here, the one-and-a-half-story cypress and pine cottage illustrates the type of modest, yet comfortable, dwelling built by Lowcountry planters who spent most of their time in their more opulent town houses in Charleston .

Cottage – The rectangular plan, side gable roof and wide front porch of the modest c.1828 home you see here now are all elements shared by 19C coastal cottages. Inside, there's no furniture, but informative panels describe Pinckney's life and his career as a statesman, which included three terms as South Carolina governor, one term in the US Senate, and a four-year stint as ambassador to Spain under President Thomas Jefferson.

Grounds – Roam the grounds to discover the archaeological research underway here. To date, scientists have found the vestiges of a detached kitchen, a privy, and a slave village. The latter reveals a wealth of information for anyone interested in the area's African-American heritage.

"Constitution Charlie"

An often forgotten founding father and son of a wealthy planter, **Charles Cotesworth Pinckney** (1746–1825) is one of four Charlestonians who went to Philadelphia in May 1787 to help draft the new Constitution of the United States. Prior to leaving, Pinckney and John Rutledge wrote a version of the Constitution, which they later presented to the convention. More than 30 provisions mentioned in "the Pinckney Draught" were incorporated into the final Constitution; these included eliminating religious testing as a qualification for holding public office, assigning impeachment power to the House of Representatives, and establishing a single chief executive. Disliked by James Madison—whose journals provide the best source of information about the convention—the pompous Pinckney never received the credit he deserved for his contributions. Since his personal papers were later destroyed by fire, no records survive today to tell Pinckney's side of the story.

Plantations

Boone Hall Plantation

1235 Long Point Rd., Mt. Pleasant. 7mi north of Charleston via US-17 North. Turn left on Long Point Rd.; Boone Hall is across the street from Charles Pinckney National Historic Site. 843-884-4371. www.boonehallplantation.com. Open Apr–Labor Day Mon–Sat 8:30am–6:30pm, Sun 1pm–4pm. Rest of the year Mon–Sat 9am–5pm, Sun 1pm–5pm. Closed Thanksgiving Day & Dec 25. $14.50.

You'll feel like Scarlett O'Hara as you drive up the romantic half-mile avenue lined by centuries-old moss-draped live oaks leading to Boone Hall (Scarlett, of course, would have traveled by horse-drawn carriage).

Built in the 1700s, this former cotton plantation is named for Major John Boone, who acquired the deed to the 17,000 acres of land in 1681 from the Lord Proprietors of the Carolina colony. Today visitors are welcome on the remaining 738 acres, which also host many public and private events, as well as serving as a popular film location.

Mansion – *Visit by 30-minute guided tour only.* Constructed in 1935, the Colonial Revival-style main house respects the design of the original mid-18C structure, which was destroyed by fire. Guides in hoop skirts take you through the first-floor rooms, pointing out such treasures as the mahogany Hepplewhite dining room table and the English Royal Crown Darby china trimmed in 24-karat gold.

Grounds – Located behind the Avenue of the Oaks, you'll find a group of unrestored slave cabins dating back to 1743. The cabins, along with the smokehouse and cotton gin on the grounds, were made with brick produced on the plantation. The formal gardens contain varieties of antique roses dating back to the 16C.

Boone Hall Farm

Boone Hall is still a working farm, and you can sample its bounty nearly year-round. In spring, come pick strawberries; in summer there are peaches and tomatoes. October brings pumpkins and hayrides, and in December you can buy fresh-cut Fraser firs. *Call or check Web site for hours and fees.*

Carolina Gold

Luckily for the area's early economy, rice was well-suited to the Lowcountry's hot, humid climate. The crop first came to Carolina from Madagascar by way of slaves, who brought the grains and the knowledge of how to plant them. With its golden hull and fine quality, this particular variety of African rice became known as "Carolina Gold." Shipped to markets throughout Europe, rice ruled as South Carolina's most important product up until the Civil War.

Although the colonists' first attempts at growing rice failed, by 1726 the crop was being grown near tidal rivers where fields could be flooded and later drained. It wasn't easy to cultivate rice. Nearly every task associated with rice growing had to be done by hand, from clearing the land to digging the dikes and ditches that would divert river water to the fields, and, finally, milling the rice itself.

These tasks, of course, fell to the slaves, who served as the backbone of the plantations. In the mid-18C, slaves were expected to clear 1,200 square feet of land a day and hand-thresh 600 sheaves of rice. Using sticks called "flails," they beat the rice stalks until the grains fell out; then they separated the grains from the shafts by shaking them in large, flat winnowing baskets. Rice was milled by hand using a mortar and pestle to remove the tough outer husk.

For nearly 200 years, the 300-mile coastline from Cape Fear, North Carolina, to the St. Marys River in Georgia, reigned as the "Kingdom of Rice." In the years leading up to the Civil War, South Carolina alone counted 227 plantations—encompassing a whopping 70,000 acres of land—in cultivation, which produced an average of 11 million pounds of rice a year. Their fortunes assured by the 1840s, rice-plantation owners became gentlemen of leisure, spending much of their time socializing in their fine Charleston town houses, and managing their estates from afar.

After the Civil War, planters couldn't afford to pay workers to do the back-breaking labor—once performed by slaves—that growing rice required. Without free labor, it was too costly to try and cultivate rice, and planters gradually turned to other means of support, such as growing cotton and mining phosphate along the rivers.

Lowcountry Plantations

There are a couple of plantations that lie a bit farther away from Charleston (within an hour's drive), and you can visit them on your way up to **Myrtle Beach★**. *For descriptions, see The Grand Strand.*

Hopsewee Plantation – *494 Hopsewee Rd., Georgetown. 48mi north of Charleston on US-17 North.*

Hampton Plantation State Park – *1950 Rutledge Rd., McClellanville. 47.5mi north of Charleston via US-17 North; turn left on Rutledge Rd.*

Fun Fact

In the late 18C, the wealthy class in Charles Towne was so crazy about rice that local cabinetmakers created the "rice bed," carved with rice ears and leaves on its bedposts—a popular style that's still reproduced today.

Beaches

Grab your towel and sunscreen and head for wide expanses of sand that line the coast north and south of Charleston. From residential Isle of Palms to tony Kiawah, Charleston's barrier-island beaches make a great excursion. Whether you spend the day at one of the area's public beach parks or stay longer at an island resort, you're sure to find fun in the sun that the whole family will enjoy.

Public Beach Parks
Beachwalker County Park

21mi south of Charleston. 1 Beachwalker Dr., on the southern end of Kiawah Island. From Charleston, take the James Island Connector and turn right on Folly Rd. Go left on Maybank Hwy. (Rte. 700) to Bohicket Rd. Turn left on Bohicket Rd. and follow signs to Kiawah Island. Turn left on Kiawah Island Pkwy. and take the first right on Beachwalker Dr. 843-768-2395. www.ccprc.com. Open May–Labor Day daily 9am–7pm. Sept daily 10am–6pm. Apr & Oct weekends only 10am–6pm. Mar weekends only 10am–5pm. Closed Nov–Feb. $5/vehicle.

If you want to experience the spectacular beach on **Kiawah Island**★★ *(see The Lowcountry Coast)*, but don't want to rent accommodations on the private resort, spend a day at Beachwalker Park. Located just outside the resort's gates, the county park offers equipment rentals, lifeguards (in summer), dressing areas, outdoor showers, restrooms, and picnic areas outfitted with grills. For supplies, there's a convenience store and gas station right on Beachwalker Drive as you turn off Kiawah Island Parkway.

Folly Beach County Park

12mi south of Charleston. 1010 West Ashley Ave., on the west end of Folly Island. Take the James Island Connector (Rte. 30) to Folly Rd. Turn left on Folly Rd. and continue 8mi until it ends. Turn right at the light at Ashley Ave. and follow it to the end. 843-588-2426. www.ccprc.com. Open May–Labor Day daily 9am–7pm. Apr, Sept & Oct daily 9am–6pm. Nov–Mar daily 10am–5pm. $5/vehicle (no fee Nov–Feb).

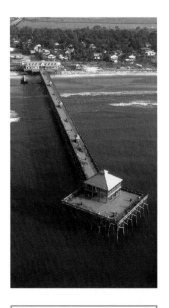

The closest sands to Charleston, bohemian Folly Beach caters to hordes of locals and visitors. Rent an umbrella and some chairs and stake out your spot along the 2,500 feet of oceanfront. The park offers the same amenities as Beachwalker Park, as well as a snack bar and boogie-board rentals in case the kids forgot their own boards. In summer, lifeguards patrol a designated beach area.

Nearby Folly Beach **fishing pier** invites avid anglers to drop a line and see what's biting *(see Musts for Outdoor Fun)*. The biggest fish ever caught from the pier was a 100-pound tarpon in 1996.

Folly or Folly? – The label Folly Beach originally came from the Old English word meaning "dense foliage," which is likely what the early settlers found along the coast here. Today, though, the tiny beach town with its carefree attitude identifies more with the modern definition of the word.

Touring Tip

Parking is scant at this county park, which draws throngs of sunseekers on nice summer weekends. Plan to come early if you want a good space.

Beer-drinkers take note: No alcoholic beverages are permitted on any of the county beaches.

McKevlin's Surf Shop

8 Center St. 843-588-2247. www.mckevlins.com. One of the oldest surf shops on the East Coast, McKevlin's was established in 1965 by local surfer Dennis McKevlin and his eldest son, Ted. Today the shop boasts 3,300 square feet of retail space filled with surfboards, bodyboards, wax, and car racks. Even if you're not a surfer, it's always cool to have a McKevlin's T-shirt.

• For the latest on where the best waves are breaking, call McKevlin's **Surf Report**: 843-588-2261.

Sea Turtle Season

Loggerhead sea turtles *(Caretta caretta)* nest along the coast of South Carolina each year from mid-May through October. Females will dig a nest in the sand, where they lay up to 150 ping-pong-ball-size eggs that will incubate for 54 to 60 days. After emerging from their eggs at night, the hatchlings instinctively move away from the shadows and seek the brightest horizon—normally the ocean. Glaring lights of beach-front development confuse the young turtles, who often head in the wrong direction, decreasing their chances of survival.

The **South Carolina Aquarium**★★ *(see Musts for Kids)* sponsors a sea turtle "head start" program to help this threatened species (all species of sea turtles are either endangered or threatened). Each summer, the aquarium acquires a few loggerhead hatchlings from local beaches and raises them in protected conditions for a couple of years before releasing them into the ocean.

Several areas, including Kiawah Island and Folly Beach, have organized groups that patrol the beaches and fence off the turtle nests so that beachgoers don't inadvertently destroy them. If you see signs of turtle activity, please be sure not to disturb the nests.

What's So Cool about Loggerhead Sea Turtles?

- Loggerheads can live up to 50 years or more.
- Female turtles return to lay their eggs on or near the same beach where they hatched.
- Adult loggerheads can weigh anywhere from 170 to 500 pounds; their shell, called a carapace, can grow up to 45 inches in length.
- Loggerheads are carnivorous; they use their powerful jaws to devour a variety of fish and shellfish.
- Loggerhead sea turtles have been officially listed as a threatened species since 1978.

Isle of Palms County Park

12mi northeast of Charleston. 1-14th Aves., Isle of Palms (between Palm Blvd. & Ocean Blvd.). Take US-17 North to the Isle of Palms Connector (Rte. 517). When the connector ends at Palm Blvd., go straight through the light and follow signs. 843-886-3863. www.ccprc.com. Open May–Labor Day daily 9am–7pm. Apr, Sept & Oct daily 9am–6pm. Nov–Mar daily 10am–5pm. $5/vehicle (no fee Nov–Feb).

A 25-minute drive north of downtown, six-mile-long **Isle of Palms** makes a great escape from the city's often-crowded streets. This is a real beach community, with a large year-round population. Besides lifeguards (in summer) and all the other amenities found at Folly Beach and Beachwalker Park, Isle of Palms County Park has a children's play area and a sand volleyball court. Just behind the beach you'll find a recently spruced-up commercial strip featuring metered parking, shops, beachfront bars *(see p 115)*, and an outpost of Ben and Jerry's ice cream *(closed in winter)*.

The pier here is not open to the public.

● **Best Surfing** – From the pier up to 30th Street.

Beach Rentals

Prices for rentals at all three county beach parks: 1 chair, $8/day; 1 umbrella $8/day; or save a few bucks by renting 2 chairs and 1 umbrella for $20/day. If you come after 4pm, when the crowds start to leave, rental fees drop to $5 for one chair or one umbrella.

Beach Resorts

For descriptions of individual beach resorts, see The Grand Strand and The Lowcountry Coast.

The Grand Strand★★

Myrtle Beach is 98mi north of Charleston via US-17.

The excitement of **Myrtle Beach**★ and the quieter Grand Strand resort areas of Litchfield Beach and Pawleys Island, are less than a two-hour drive north of Charleston.

Kiawah Island★★

21mi south of Charleston via US-17.

A luxury resort with amenities galore tucks into the marshland and maritime forest on the island of Kiawah.

Wild Dunes★

15mi north of Charleston on Isle of Palms.

This golf and tennis resort occupies the northern tip of Isle of Palms.

Shelling on the Coast

Despite the fact that Blackbeard once prowled South Carolina's shore, the buried treasure you're most likely to find on these beaches is of the mollusk variety. Hunting for seashells can provide hours of fun for both kids and their parents. The wealth of seashells you might uncover at low tide—the best time to hunt for shells—includes fuzzy gray sand dollars, striped lightening whelks, snail-like baby's ears, colorful calico scallops, long, slender augers, and Atlantic clams.

Remember one rule of thumb: Never take shells with live creatures in them; you don't want to disturb some critter's home!

Parks and Gardens

With its semi-tropical climate, Charleston flowers year-round with a splashy variety of blooms from camellias and winter jessamine *(Jan–Feb)* to azaleas and magnolias *(Apr–May)* to roses and crape myrtles *(Jun–Aug)*. And since it's warm out more months than not here, you can enjoy the city's parks and gardens in every season.

Peninsula Parks

Waterfront Park ★

Cumberland St. to Tradd St. 843-724-7327. www.ci.charleston.sc.us.

Set along Charleston Harbor, in the heart of the historic district, this eight-acre linear park occupies the space once filled by the warehouses and wharves of the old port. It's often identified by the fanciful **pineapple fountain** at its center. In warm weather—which is most of the year in Charleston—kids love to run through the **circular fountain** by the pier (at the end of Vendue Range). Joggers and walkers favor the paved walkway that runs along the water-  front, and the park's spacious green lawns make a great place for a picnic *(see Musts for Fun)*. Arranged on the inland side of the park, small landscaped "garden rooms" provide peaceful places for outdoor reading or quiet contemplation.

Pier – *Entrance at the end of Vendue Range.* The pleasant 400-foot pier juts out into the harbor and provides picnic tables and wooden swings for taking in the water views. You can even bring your rod and reel and see what's biting.

Glorious Gardens

843-722-3405. www.historiccharleston.org. $45. Held every Thursday during the annual **Festival of Homes and Gardens** *(mid-Mar–mid-Apr; see p 86)*, Glorious Gardens self-guided walking tours take you inside the gates of as many as 12 private gardens in the historic district during the city's peak blooming season. Here you'll see plots bright with azaleas, dogwoods, magnolias, jasmine, tea olives and other spring blossoms; after the tour, there's a reception in the garden of the Nathaniel Russell House *(51 Meeting St.; see Historic District)*.

White Point Gardens★

Along the Battery, at the intersection of East Bay St. & Murray Blvd. 843-724-7327.
www.ci.charleston.sc.us.

Named for the gleaming white oyster beds that the first settlers found on this site in 1670, White Point occupies the southern tip of Charleston's peninsula. It was here that the settlers relocated their fledgling town in 1680.

This strategic point at the junction of the Ashley and Cooper rivers was used to defend the city as far back as the early 1700s, when the original walls were built around the new town. Established as a public park in 1837, White Point was again used as a gun battery during the Civil War. A number of Confederate cannons still stand in the park as reminders of less peaceful times. Monuments here honor heroes from the Revolutionary War and the Civil War, including the crew of the *H.L. Hunley (see Historic Sites).*

White Point Gallows

In its early days, Charles Towne was plagued by pirates, including the notorious Edward Teach, aka "Blackbeard," who captured several ships in Charleston Harbor in 1718. But perhaps Charleston's most famous roque was Stede Bonnet, the well-educated son of a wealthy Barbadian family who turned to piracy after serving as a major in the Barbados army. Whether Bonnet became a pirate to escape his wife's incessant nagging, as legend has it, or whether his whim "proceeded from a disorder of his mind," as his cronies believed, remains anyone's guess.

Called the "gentleman pirate" for his cultured manner, Bonnet took part in Blackbeard's siege of Charleston Harbor. In 1718 Bonnet was captured on the Cape Fear River, in North Carolina and brought back to Charleston to stand trial for his crimes. Despite his gentlemanly behavior, Bonnet was sentenced to hang in White Point Gardens—along with another 49 pirates who met the same fate later that year (Bonnet's letter pleading for his life is on display in the Old Provost Dungeon; *see Historic Sites*). A plaque in the park commemorates Bonnet and the other pirates who met their end in White Point Gardens.

The gracious four-block-long park that you see today was laid out in 1906 by John Charles Olmsted (stepson of renowned landscape architect Frederick Law Olmsted, whose credits include New York's Central Park). Also referred to simply as The Battery *(see Historic District)*, White Point Gardens makes a wonderful spot for strolling, picnicking *(see Musts for Fun)* or just relaxing amid its palmettos and moss-draped live oak trees. Of course, the expansive view out to the horizon is not bad, either!

Hampton Park

Entrance on Cleveland St., off Rutledge Ave. 843-724-7327. www.ci.charleston.sc.us.

Just outside the Citadel's gates and bounded by Mary Murray Drive, Hampton Park embraces

60 acres of lovely recreational space, including a lake, a rose garden, a concert bandstand, and trails for walking, biking or jogging.

Kids Run

One of Charleston's biggest athletic events is the **Cooper River Bridge Run**, held every April *(see p 98)*. For years, the event's sponsors have hosted a Kids Run the day before the adult race. In 2004, the Kids Run moved to Hampton Park and turned into a whole afternoon of fun. Kids of all ages are invited to participate; the festivities start with a 25-yard dash for toddlers and go up to a 1-mile run for ages 8 to 13. Even if your little ones don't want to run, they can still climb the rock wall, visit the petting zoo and play on the jump castle and super slide. *Registration is required for the race: $8 with T-shirt, free without T-shirt; 843-792-0345; www.bridgerun.com.*

West Ashley Gardens

Middleton Place Gardens★★★

4300 Ashley River Rd. 843-556-6020. www.middletonplace.org. Open year-round daily 9am–5pm. Closed Thanksgiving Day & Dec 25. General admission (gardens & grounds) $20 adults, $5 children (free for children under age 6). See Plantations.

America owes its oldest landscaped gardens to moneyed plantation owner Henry Middleton, who laid them out in classic European style in 1741. The main sight line slopes down from the entrance gates over terraces above the twin "butterfly" ponds (shaped like two butterfly wings) to the Ashley River just beyond. More than 100 slaves spent 10 years digging ornamental canals, planting shrubs and forming the land according to Middleton's elaborate plan. In keeping with 18C ideals of what a garden should be, his plan called for symmetrical "galleries" to be walled in by greenery, and views to reach down to the river across wide, grassy lawns.

Opened to the public in the 1920s, Middleton's masterpiece has been added to over the years; new plantings now color the original plan, so that the gardens bloom 12 months of the year.

Camellia Walks at Middleton Place

From February to mid-March, Middleton Place sponsors special guided walks that spotlight its prized collection of lovely camellias. Of the hundreds of varieties planted here, the oldest camellia dates back to 1786. Tours last 1 ½ hours and are held on selected days *(call or check Web site for schedule)* beginning at 11am. Reservations are required.

Magnolia Plantation★★

3550 Ashley River Rd. 843-571-1266. www.magnoliaplantation.com. Open Mar–Oct daily 8am–5:30pm. Rest of the year daily 8am–5pm. $13 adults, $7 children (ages 6-12). See Plantations.

Azaleas rule. At least they do at Magnolia's 50 acres of gardens from mid-March through April, when some 250 different varieties of azaleas paint the canal banks in vibrant pink, white and purple. Then there are the twisting wisteria vines dripping with clusters of lavender flowers, delicate yellow forsythia, fragrant honeysuckle and pink and white dogwoods—don't forget your camera!

In summer you'll find magnolias—of course—along with lilies and wildflowers. Fall and winter are when the 900 types of camellias flower; more than 150 of them were developed here on the plantation.

Garden Highlights

After Reverend John Grimke Drayton inherited Magnolia Plantation in 1820, he developed the existing gardens, enhancing the natural landscape, rather than creating a formal garden such as the one at Middleton Place. He is credited with introducing the first *Azalea Indica* to America in the mid-19C.

- **Long White Bridge** – Rev. Drayton built this graceful arched garden landmark in the 1840s to span a natural river marsh.

- **Biblical Garden** – What plants might have grown in the Garden of Eden? You'll find some of the answers in this educational plot.

- **Barbados Tropical Garden** – Since the original owner of the plantation hailed from Barbados, it's only fitting that the plantation displays some of that island's flora.

- **Maze** – Kids—and adults—will love getting lost in this labyrinth, modeled on the boxwood maze that King Henry VIII designed for his country estate in the 16C. Instead of using the boxwood, though, this maze is fashioned from camellias and hollies. See if you can find your way out!

Bird Walk

Birders, take note: every Sunday morning at 8:30am, Magnolia Plantation sponsors a guided bird walk to see some of the 224 species that have been spotted here. You might observe great blue herons, anhingas, egrets, coots, gallinules and bald eagles during the three-hour tour. Meet in the main parking lot by the antebellum cabin. Tickets are $12 and include basic admission to the garden and grounds.

Audubon Swamp Garden★

At Magnolia Gardens, 3550 Ashley River Rd. 843-571-1266. www.magnoliaplantation.com/ swampgarden. Open Mar–Oct daily 8am–5:30pm. Rest of the year daily 8am–5pm. $5 adults, $4 children (ages 6-12).

Covering an eerie 60 acres of black-water cypress and tupelo swamp, this area was added to Magnolia Plantation in the 1980s. It takes its name from early-19C naturalist John James Audubon, who visited Magnolia Plantation to study waterbirds during one of his many trips to Charleston.

Allow at least an hour to wander the boardwalks and bridges through the swamp and give yourself ample time to drink in the colors and textures of the place: brilliant green duckweed that makes the water appear solid, knobby

Swamp Thing

The murky water of Audubon Swamp Garden made a fitting setting for the 1982 horror flick, *The Swamp Thing*, starring Louis Jourdan and Adrienne Barbeau.

black silhouettes of cypress knees, lacy ferns and bright lilies. Keep your eye out for wildlife along the way. White ibis, blue-winged teals, great blue herons and snowy egrets are just a tiny sampling of the more than 200 types of birds that have been seen at Audubon Swamp Gardens. That's not to mention otters, turtles and, of course, alligators, the ever-present denizens of the swamp.

Beach and County Parks

Whether you're beaching it or not, try one of these area county parks, most of which are open to the public daily year-round *(www.ccprc.com)*.

Beachwalker County Park – *1 Beachwalker Dr., Kiawah Island.* This county park on otherwise private Kiawah Island is open March through October. *See Beaches.*

Folly Beach County Park – *1010 West Ashley Ave., at the south end of Folly Rd.* Charleston's beach packs in the crowds on summer weekends. *See Beaches.*

Isle of Palms County Park – *1-14th Aves., Isle of Palms.* A 25-minute drive north of Charleston brings you to this wide public beach. *See Beaches.*

James Island County Park – *871 Riverland Dr., on James Island.* OK, this one's not a beach, but it's still lots of fun for the whole family. *See Musts for Kids.*

Angel Oak

3688 Angel Oak Rd., Johns Island. From Charleston, take the James Island connector to Folly Rd. and turn right; turn left on Maybank Hwy./Rte. 700 and take it to Bohicket Rd. (follow signs for Kiawah Island). Turn left on Bohicket Rd. and follow signs to Angel Oak (on the right). www.angeloaktree.org.

It's rare to find a tree that's outlived logging, hurricanes and earthquakes, but this live oak *(Quercus virginiana)* has done just that. Estimated to be 1,400 years old, the 65-foot-high Angel Oak spreads its branches 160 feet around. It's worth a drive—especially if you're headed to Kiawah Island *(see The Lowcountry Coast)*—to see this ancient oak. Pack a picnic when you come; even on the hottest summer day, Angel Oak shades an area of 17,000 square feet.

Museums

Charleston may not harbor a lot of museums, but the handful it does have are well worth a look. Take a sailor's-eye view of maritime history at Patriots Point; peek at Lowcountry artistic traditions at the Gibbes Museum; and travel back through time at the Charleston Museum.

Patriots Point Naval & Maritime Museum★★

3mi north of Charleston in Mt. Pleasant. Take US-17 North across the bridge and follow signs for Rte. 703. Take the first right on Patriots Point Rd. 843-884-2727. www.patriotspoint.org. Open Apr–Sept 9am–7:30pm. Rest of the year 9am–6:30pm. Closed Dec 25. $14 adults, $7 children (ages 6-11). Free for children under age 6.

Touring Tip

Allow at least two hours—although you could easily spend longer—to explore the *Yorktown* and the other ships. Scrambling up and down through the decks of the *Yorktown* can be tricky; access is by ladder-like stairways, and requires a certain amount of agility. Patriots Point is one of the two places that you can catch a boat to **Fort Sumter**★★★; the other is at Aquarium Wharf *(see Historic Sites)*. For schedules, call 843-884-2727.

You may have wondered what that huge gray shape is across the harbor from Charleston. It's the World War II aircraft carrier the **USS Yorktown**★★, centerpiece of Patriots Point. Built to honor the men and women who have served the US Navy in the 20C, Patriots Point features four historic vessels, a mock-up of a US Navy base camp in Vietnam, and the Cold War Submarine Memorial *(across the parking lot on Charleston Harbor)*.

Dubbed the "Fighting Lady," the *Yorktown* was commissioned in Newport News, Virginia, in 1943. During World War II, she carried a crew of 380 officers and 3,038 enlisted men, along with 90 aircraft on board. After the war she served in Vietnam, and later recovered the astronauts from Apollo 8 when they returned from their moon orbit in 1968. The *Yorktown* was decommissioned in 1970; the ship was towed from New Jersey to Charleston five years later.

You're free to roam this vast, 888-foot-long floating museum from engine room to bridge, following any of six self-guided tours that take you through five lower decks and seven levels above the hangar bay. In all you'll find 25 naval aircraft on board, some in the hangar bay, others up on the flight deck.

Three additional World War II ships are berthed at Patriots Point:

- **Clamagore** World War II submarine
- **Laffey** DD724 Destroyer
- **Ingham** Coast Guard cutter

Charleston Museum★

360 Meeting St. 843-722-2996. www.charlestonmuseum.org. Open year-round Mon–Sat 9am–5pm, Sun 1pm–5pm. Closed major holidays. $9 adults, $5 children (ages 3-12). Combination tickets are available for the museum and the Heyward-Washington and Joseph Manigault houses, which the museum also operates (see Historic District).

Located across the street from the visitor center, the Charleston Museum is a good place to begin your tour of the city. Exhibits in this contemporary brick structure cover Charleston and the Lowcountry's social and natural history from pre-settlement days to the present. The scope of the museum's collection ranges from a prehistoric crocodile skeleton to a scale model of the *Pioneer* Civil War-era submarine.

What's What in the Museum?

The South Carolina Lowcountry – The museum's largest permanent exhibit begins with the area's geology and earliest native inhabitants. It tells the story of Charleston from its first settlers, through the Revolution and the city's plantation heyday, to the Civil War and Reconstruction, and finally to the 20C. Objects, including Revolutionary War swords, sweet grass baskets used to process rice, and Victorian furnishings, illustrate each period in the city's long history.

The Early Days – An Egyptian mummy and a giant taxidermed polar bear might not have much connection to the Lowcountry, but these number among the natural-history artifacts from the original museum, which was located nearby in Thompson Auditorium. Founded in 1773, the old museum gave Charlestonians a "window on the world" through its collection of casts of ancient Roman statues, scientific specimens and skeletons of prehistoric animals.

Charleston Silver – The museum's holdings of 18C and 19C silver made in Charleston reflect the changing tastes of Charleston society over the years. George Washington's christening cup is one of the collection's treasures.

Charleston Museum for Kids

History isn't always boring; kids are bound to find something to interest them here. Check out the for Kids Tours, each Wednesday in June and July at 3:30pm. This free, guided tour focuses on a particular artifact in the museum's collection, such as the Egyptian mummy or the dinosaur skeleton. Kids will also get to do activities or crafts projects related to the object being highlighted on the tour.

Gibbes Museum of Art★

*135 Meeting St. 843-722-2706. www.gibbes.com. Open year-round Tue–Sat 10am–5pm,
Sun 1pm–5pm. Closed Mon & major holidays. $7.*

American art with a "Charleston perspective"—that's what you'll find at the
Gibbes. Most of the more than 15,000 objects in the museum, which opened in

1905, showcase works that have some
connection to the Lowcountry,
whether they were created in
Charleston, done by local artists,
collected by the city's residents, or
simply portray life in the Charleston
area. The permanent collection occupies the first floor; most of the gallery
space on the second floor contains
changing exhibits.

Art in the South—The Charleston Perspective – This collection of more than
500 paintings focuses on 18C, 19C and 20C American art by the likes of Ben-
jamin West, Gilbert Stuart, Thomas Sully, and Henrietta Johnston, who's hailed
as America's first professional female artist. Included in this group of paintings
are works by Charleston Renaissance artists Elizabeth O'Neill Verner, Alice
Ravenel Huger Smith and Anna Heyward Taylor.

Rice Plantation Series – In 1937 artist
Alice Ravenel Huger Smith (1876–1958)
donated 30 original watercolors to the
museum; these paintings now make up
one of the museum's most significant
collections.

Miniature Portrait Collection – The
museum's 600 examples of tiny paintings,
conceived as tokens of affection, encom-
pass works by English, French and American artists. They span the years from
the 18C through the early 20C.

The Charleston Renaissance

Charleston's renaissance was a cultural one. In the mid-1920s, the city of Charleston
found itself down in the mouth. Its grand antebellum mansions were literally crumbling; its economy was depressed. Enter a group of local artists and writers, who
sought to bring attention to the city's rich cultural heritage. Writer DuBose
Heyward—who penned the 1925 book *Porgy*, on which composer George Gershwin
based his folk opera *Porgy and Bess* in 1935; and Charleston painter Elizabeth O'Neill
Verner, along with many others, all interpreted the Lowcountry folkways in their art.
Through their music, books and canvases, they created images of the daily life of
Charleston and the nearby plantations for the world to see. The cultural renewal they
launched, which became known as the Charleston Renaissance, emphasized American
values and realism; the sense of civic pride it fostered would eventually fuel
Charleston's historic-preservation movement *(see p 33)*.

American Military Museum

360 Concord St., in ground floor of the IMAX building. 843-577-7000. www.americanmilitary museum.org. Open year-round Mon–Sat 10am–6pm, Sun 1pm–5pm. Closed Thanksgiving Day & Dec 25. $6 ($5 for veterans).

In its new space next to Aquarium Wharf, the museum fills 7,000 square feet with uniforms, weaponry, medals, and personal artifacts belonging to soldiers from all branches of the US military service. Exhibits are arranged chronologically beginning with the present—the Iraq conflict—and going back to the Revolutionary War. There's even a case full of miniature soldiers that will appeal to the young at heart.

Children's Museum of the Lowcountry – *25 Ann St. See Musts for Kids.*

The Citadel Museum – *On The Citadel campus. See Historic Sites.*

Confederate Museum

188 Meeting St., at the corner of Market St. 843-723-1541. Open year-round Tue–Sat 11am–3:30pm. Closed Sun, Mon & major holidays. $5.

Established by the Daughters of the Confederacy in 1898, this collection in Market Hall *(second floor; see Historic Sites)* contains an important group of artifacts and archives of documents from the Civil War, including uniforms, weapons, flags and historic photographs.

House Museums

Charleston is renowned for its splendid house museums, which will give you a taste of how the city's wealthy planters lived. Here's a list of the house museums described in this guide. *See Historic District for detailed descriptions.*

Nathaniel Russell House★★★ – *51 Meeting St. Visit by 30-minute guided tour only. 843-724-8481. www.historiccharleston.org.*

Aiken-Rhett House★★ – *48 Elizabeth St. Visit by 30-minute guided tour only. 843-724-8481. www.historiccharleston.org.*

Edmondston-Alston House★★ – *21 East Battery. Visit by 30-minute guided tour only. 843-722-7171. www.middletonplace.org.*

Heyward-Washington House★★ – *87 Church St. Visit by 30-minute guided tour only. 843-722-2996. www.charlestonmuseum.org.*

Joseph Manigault House★ – *350 Meeting St., across from Charleston Museum. Visit by 30-minute guided tour only. 843-722-2996. www.charlestonmuseum.org.*

Despite its mannerly exterior, Charleston isn't above laughing at itself. In fact, the Holy City likes to let its hair down once in a while for some good old-fashioned fun. Here are some quintessentially Charleston things to do.

Carriage Tours

It would be a shame to visit Charleston and not clip-clop around the historic district in one of the horse- or mule-drawn carriages that share the city's downtown streets with more modern vehicles. The carriage rides are a wonderful way to get an overview of the historic district. Along the way, your driver/guide will provide a witty—though not always historically accurate—narration of local history and lore.

There are a number of different companies that provide carriage tours. Choose the one that appeals to you by checking out the lineup along Anson and North Market streets, near the Old City Market.

Tours last one hour and costs average around $18 for adults and $10 for children. Here are a few of the classics:

- **Classic Carriage Tours** – *10 Guignard St. 843-853-3747. www.classiccarriage.com.*

- **Old South Carriage Company** – *14 Anson St. 843-723-9712. www.oldsouthcarriage.com.*

- **Palmetto Carriage Tours** – *40 N. Market St. 843-723-8145. www.carriagetour.com.*

Drinks with a View

Charleston may not have many high-rise buildings, but that doesn't mean there's no place for panoramic vistas. Here are a few rooftops where the cognoscenti go for cocktails.

Market Pavilion Bar – *Top floor of the Market Pavilion Hotel, 225 East Bay St., at the corner of Market St. 843-723-7320. www.marketpavilion.com. Open Sun–Thu 11:30am–midnight, Fri & Sat 11am–2am.* The historic district's rooftops and the harbor stretch out below you as you relax at this chic Charleston hot spot. Grab a table or a seat at the bar near the hotel's cascading pool and order a cocktail, or perhaps nibble an appetizer from the light-fare menu. Go before dinner to watch the sunset and sip an aperitif, or stop by later for a brandy and dessert.

Roof Top Bar and Restaurant – *Top floor of the Vendue Inn, 19 Vendue Range, off East Bay St. 843-577-7970. www.vendueinn.com. Open daily 11:30am–11pm.* Charleston's original rooftop bar offers great views along with appetizers. You can listen to live music here Sunday through Friday nights *(6:30pm–9:30pm)*.

Terrace at Marion Square

372 King St., on top of Millennium Music at the corner of Calhoun St. (take the elevator to the third floor). 843-937-0314. www.terracerestaurants.com. Open Mon–Sat 11:30am–11pm, Sun 11am–2:30pm.

This rooftop hangout may cater to the College of Charleston crowd, but it's more than just a student hangout. The Terrace makes a great place to start or end your trek down King Street or your tour of the College of Charleston—there's even a Blue Jean Brunch on Sunday. Tasty appetizers include fried olives and sautéed Carolina lump crab cakes; you can choose among salads, sandwiches, pizzas, steak and seafood on the diverse menu of entrées. Don't let a little bad weather stop you from coming here—on cool evenings, suspended heat lamps will keep you warm, and plastic curtains drop down to shelter the rooftop when it rains.

Musts For Fun

Ghostly Charleston

Face it, a city as old as Charleston is bound to have its share of ghosts. And Charleston does, if you believe the local lore. You can meet—hopefully not face to face!—some of the city's favorite spirits on one of the following ghost tours. Leave the little ones at home and take to Charleston's venerable streets and cemeteries with a guide after dark for an eerie adventure. You'll be scared you did!

The 90-minute walking tours listed below all require reservations (call for schedule). Due to the potentially frightening nature of the subject matter, children under age 7 are not permitted on ghost tours.

The Ghosts of Charleston – *Tours depart from Waterfront Park, at the end of Vendue Range. 843-723-1670. www.tourcharleston.com. $15 adults, $10 children (ages 7-14).* Aside from a spooky walk through the historic district, this company offers another tour (Ghosts II) that takes in the edges of town *(departs from Marion Square).*

The Lady in White

If you happen to be wandering around the eerie tree-shrouded graveyard of Charleston's Unitarian Church *(4 Archdale St.)* at night, keep an eye out for the city's most frequently seen ghost, known as the "Lady in White." According to Julian T. Buxton, author of *The Ghosts of Charleston*, the spirit of Mary Bloomfield White (died 1907) haunts the churchyard here searching for her husband, whose plot next to hers lies empty. Her partner died on the same date as Mary did, 500 miles away, in Baltimore, Maryland. To this day, no one knows the location of his grave. For the rest of the story, check out Buxton's book or take the Ghosts of Charleston tour *(above)* given by Tour Charleston.

Lowcountry Ghost Walk – *Tours depart from 58 ¹/₂ Broad St. nightly 5:30pm, 7:30pm & 9:30pm (except Jan 1 & Dec 25) . 800-729-3420. www.charlestonwalks.com. $15 adults, $8 children (ages 7-14).* Plan to walk a little over a mile on this tour.

Ghost and Dungeon Walking Tour – *Tours depart from 40 N. Market St., nightly 7pm & 9pm. 843-722-8687. www.charlestondungeon.com. $17 adults, $8 children (ages 7-12).* The tour includes a walk through Charleston's Provost Dungeon *(see Historic District).*

Musts For Fun

Harbor Cruises

Cruising the rivers around the Charleston peninsula makes a great family excursion on a pretty day. Whether you do a harbor tour, a dinner cruise or a nature excursion, being out on the water will give you a new perspective of the city.

Here are a few places to start; you can get a complete listing of harbor tours at the Visitor Reception Center at 375 Meeting Street. Call for schedules (they vary seasonally) before you go.

SpiritLine – 843-722-2628. *www.spiritlinecruises.com. Harbor tour: $12 adults, $6 children (ages 6-11).* SpiritLine's 90-minute narrated harbor tours and 3-hour dinner cruises depart from Aquarium Wharf. They also provide service to **Fort Sumter**★★★ *(see Historic Sites).*

Outdoor Discovery Tours, Inc. – *Cruises depart from Patriots Point in Mt. Pleasant (see Museums). 888-899-1866. www.dolphin-tours.com. $18 adult, $12 children (ages 3-12).* On this 2-hour tour aboard a 30-foot pontoon boat, you're likely to see dolphins, pass a pelican rookery and learn the secrets to catching crabs.

Sandlapper Nature Tours – *Tours depart from the Maritime Center (Wharfside St., adjacent to the South Carolina Aquarium) mid-May–Sept, Sat only. 843-849-8687. www.sandlappertours.com.* This naturalist-led tour will especially appeal to both kids and nature lovers, since it includes a stop at a barrier-island beach to hunt for shells. Tide willing, the boat may even wander down a saltmarsh creek—the perfect place to spot water birds and dolphins.

Gullah Tours

Tours depart from Gallery Chuma, 43 John St. (across from the Visitor Reception Center), year-round Mon–Fri 11am & 1pm, Sat 11am, 1pm & 3pm. $18 adults, $12 children. 843-225-7551 (reservations requested). www.gullahtours.com.

Hop aboard an air-conditioned bus for an introduction to Charleston's rich African-American heritage, including the intriguing Gullah culture *(see p 144).* See Catfish Row, the setting of *Porgy and Bess*, meet sweet grass basket makers, and learn how the Underground Railroad operated in Charleston. You'll do all this and more on the two-hour excursion guided by local lecturer and resident Alphonso Brown.

Irvin House Vineyards

6775 Bear's Bluff Rd., Wadmalaw Island. 25mi south of Charleston via Maybank Hwy./ Rte. 700. 843-559-6867. www.charlestonwine.com. Open for tastings Thu–Sat 10am–5pm. Tours Sat at 2pm (free).

OK, so South Carolina isn't exactly known for its wine production. But here's a surprise: Muscadine grapes, native to the southeast, thrive in the Lowcountry's hot, humid climate. And, in the right hands, they make some decent wine. See for yourself at 48-acre Irvin House Vineyards, Charleston's only vineyard, set amid live oaks and flower gardens on Wadmalaw Island *(a 30-minute drive south of downtown)*. Five varieties (three reds, two whites), all priced at $10 a bottle at the winery, range in character from the dry Mullet Hall Red to the crisp, sweet white called Magnolia. The lovely labels, done by local artists, alone are worth the price.

A Taste of History

Tour departs from front of Charleston Museum, at Meeting & John Sts., Sat 9:30am–11:30am. Reservations required. 843-723-3366. www.carolinafoodpros.com. $35/person. Discounts are available if you purchase tickets at the Visitor Reception Center (375 Meeting St.), across from the museum.

Who knew history could be so delicious? At least it is during this two-hour culinary walking tour, led by local food expert and 10th-generation South Carolinian, Amanda Dew Manning. During the tour, you'll make three stops that spotlight local food artisans or food products. For example, you might stop at the Saturday farmers' market *(see Must Shop)*, where Amanda will give you a rundown on the best—and oldest, from a historical perspective—local produce. Or you might be lucky enough to go by Kennedy's Bakery *(see p 92)* for samples of their handmade breads and cakes. Wherever the tour stops that day, you're sure to come away with a first-hand taste of Charleston's foodways.

> **Touring Tip**
>
> The two-hour walking tour covers a distance of approximately 2 miles, so be sure to wear comfortable walking shoes. Wear a hat and sunscreen in the summer—Charleston's heat and humidity can be oppressive.

Lowcountry Cuisine

Named for the marshy prairies that line the low-lying South Carolina Coast north and south of Charleston, the Lowcountry is remarkable for its cuisine as well as its geography. Traditional Lowcountry cooking, like any regional cuisine, evolved using the ingredients at hand. Flavored by rice and okra that the slaves brought from West Africa; spices that came with settlers from the West Indies; grits ground from local corn; and plentiful shrimp, crab and oysters—the trilogy of shellfish caught off the coast—Charleston's sophisticated fare makes for some good eating.

You'll find all these foods featured prominently on Charleston's restaurant menus. Here are a few must-try dishes while you're in town:

- **Shrimp and grits** – Everyone seems to have their own version of this combination of local shrimp, fired up with spicy tasso ham and ladled over creamy grits. It's a staple on many menus in town.

- **She-crab soup** – Milk-based she-crab soup, a Charleston invention, is often served spiked with sherry.

- **Benne seed wafers** – This is the term African slaves used for sesame seeds, which they brought to the area from West Africa in the 17C. You'll find the sweet wafers sold all over the city; they make fitting souvenirs for your foodie friends.

Festival Fun

Beginning in January with the Oyster Festival and ending in December with a host of holiday happenings, you'll find a year-round roster of fun for all ages at Charleston's festivals.

Lowcountry Oyster Festival – *Boone Hall Plantation, Long Point Rd., off US-17 in Mt. Pleasant. 843-577-4030. www.charlestonrestaurantassociation.com/ oysterfestival.htm. $10 (children under age 10 free when accompanied by an adult).* Native Americans introduced settlers to roasted oysters in the 17C, and today the Lowcountry oyster roast is a time-honored tradition. The self-proclaimed "world's largest oyster roast" takes place each year in late January or early February (depending on the schedule of the Super Bowl) in Mt. Pleasant. When they say "large," they're not kidding: In 2004, 65,000 pounds—that's two tractor-trailor loads—of select oysters were trucked to the grounds of Boone Hall Plantation *(see Plantations)*. There's fun—and oysters—for all at the day-long fête, along with prizes for the best oyster recipe, the most oysters shucked and the most oysters eaten (the latter two in the shortest amount of time). Kids get awards for the best oyster costume.

Festival of Homes and Gardens – *Historic District. 843-722-3405. www.historiccharleston.org. $45.* Here's your chance to take a peek inside some of Charleston's elegant historic private homes. Every spring *(mid-Mar–mid-Apr)*, a host of residents open their doors to the public. During this month-long festival, which celebrated its 57th year in 2004, you can choose among several different tours (organized by street) totaling 150 private homes in 10 neighborhoods. Spring is one of Charleston's high seasons, so make reservations for this popular event well in advance.

Spoleto★★ – *Various locations around the city. 843-579-3100. www.spoletousa.org. See Performing Arts.* Playing up international performing arts, this 17-day festival beginning in late May was founded in 1977 by Maestro Gian Carlo Menotti as the counterpart to his Festival of Two Worlds in Spoleto, Italy. Spoleto's little sister, **Piccolo Spoleto**★ *(843-724-7305; www.piccolospoleto.org)*, runs concurrently with the big event and spotlights local and regional talent.

Patriots Point 4th of July Blast – *Patriots Point, off US-17 in Mt. Pleasant. 843- 884-2727. www.patriotspoint.org. Free admission.* What could be more patriotic than fireworks launched from the deck of the World War II aircraft carrier, USS *Yorktown*? Come see for yourself as Charleston celebrates the 4th of July at Patriots Point. Enjoy live bands, food, crafts, and the Kidz Zone play area from 2pm until midnight. Oh, and don't forget the main event—the fireworks start just after 9pm.

Holiday Parade of Boats – *Charleston Harbor. 843-724-7414. www.christmasincharleston.com.* Stake out your place early at one of the official designated viewing sites *(Waterfront Park; the* USS *Yorktown, at Patriots Point in Mt. Pleasant; and along the Battery)* for this Charleston holiday tradition. Held in early December, the parade features some 50 vessels, decked out with lights and holiday finery, which make their way from Mt. Pleasant down the Cooper River, and along the Battery to the Ashley River. There's even a fireworks display that lights up the sky above Castle Pinckney.

With all that water nearby and a climate that supports outdoor activity nearly year-round, the Charleston area can keep you busy golfing, swimming, fishing, paddling, playing tennis, or just lying on the beach. You decide how much—or how little—you want to do.

Beach It

Feeling lazy? The coastline north and south of Charleston is known for its lovely, wide sand beaches. Lay a towel at these area beach parks, and don't forget to bring your sunscreen *(for directions and descriptions, see Beaches)*:

• **Beachwalker County Park** – *1 Beachwalker Dr., Kiawah Island.*

• **Folly Beach County Park** – *1010 West Ashley Ave.*

• **Isle of Palms County Park** – *1-14th Aves., Isle of Palms.*

Folly Beach Surf Kayak Rodeo

Calling all kayakers! Each October Folly Beach hosts a rollicking weekend-long rodeo in the surf. Come test your skill—or pull up a beach chair and just watch—as contestants of all ages vie for prizes in the men's, women's, novice and junior divisions. In the surf competition, kayakers ride the waves in their narrow craft; judges determine the winners based on how long they ride, what kind of wave they select, their style and fancy maneuvers. There's even a hot-dog competition where experienced paddlers can strut their stuff in the ocean. *For more information, call 843-795-4386 or check online at www.ccprc.com/specialrodeo.htm.*

Go Fish

Water, water, everywhere—and that means lots of fish. Depending on the time of year, you can catch redfish, sea trout, tarpon, Spanish mackerel and jack crevalle, and more in Charleston area waters.

For **offshore** and **inshore charters**, try the following operators:

- **Carolina Clipper** – *825 Creekside Dr., on Shem Creek in Mt. Pleasant. 843-884-2992. www.carolinaclipper.com.*

- **Fin Stalker Charters** – *6 Hillcreek Blvd. 843-830-0448. www.backwaterfishing.com.*

- **Palmetto Charters LLC** – *Charleston Harbor Marina Resort, 24 Patriots Point Rd., Mt. Pleasant. 843-849-6004. www.palmetto charters.com.*

If you want to go it alone, try one of the Charleston area's **fishing piers**:

- **Folly Beach Edwin S. Taylor Fishing Pier** – *101 E. Arctic Ave., Folly Beach. 843-588-3474. www.ccprc.com. Open Apr–Oct 6am–11pm. Mar & Nov daily 8am–5pm. $8 nonresidents.*

- **Waterfront Park Pier** – *Cumberland St. to Tradd St. 843-724-7327. www.ci.charleston.sc.us. Open year-round daily 6am–midnight.*

- **James Island County Park Dock** – *871 Riverland Dr., on James Island. 843-795-7275. www.ccprc.com/jicp.htm. $1 park admission.*

> **Touring Tip:**
> **The Scoop on Fishing**
>
> Dropping your line off a pier doesn't require a fishing license, but more serious angling, both fresh- and saltwater, does. For information and fees, contact the Marine Resources Division of the South Carolina Department of Natural Resources: *843-953-9300 or www.dnr.state. sc.us/marine.*

The Charleston Angler

654 St. Andrews Blvd. (Hwy. 61). 843-571-3899. www.thecharlestonangler.com.

The first stop for area fly fishermen is The Charleston Angler. Here you'll find everything from live bait to the best names in rods—not to mention the helpful staff, who are avid anglers themselves. They'll be happy to fill you in on recent fishing conditions and catches, as well as answer any questions you might have.

Hit the Links

Whether or not Charleston is, as it claims, the site of America's first golf course, is a matter of some debate. What's not debatable, however, is that the area sports some great golf courses. Including the world-famous resort courses at Kiawah Island and Wild Dunes, the Charleston area counts some two dozen courses that are open to the public. Here are a few places to start; for a complete list of area links, check online at: *www.charlestongolfinc.com*.

Charleston Courses

Charleston National Country Club – *1360 National Dr., Mt. Pleasant. 843-884-3673. www.charlestonnationalgolf.com*. Hailed for its beauty, this Rees Jones-designed course skirts marshland and natural lagoons.

City of Charleston Golf Course – *2110 Maybank Hwy. 843-795-6517*. Opened in 1927, this well-maintained public course is just a five-minute drive from downtown.

> ### Touring Tip
>
> Kiawah and Wild Dunes resorts, as well as many Charleston hotels offer golf packages that include lodging. Ask about package rates when you make your reservations.

Dunes West Golf Club – *3535 Wando Plantation Way, Mt. Pleasant. 843-856-9000. www.golfduneswest.com*. Sister course to Wild Dunes *(opposite)*, Dunes West is located on the site of historic Lexington Plantation.

Links at Stono Ferry – *4812 Stono Links Dr., Hollywood. 843-763-1817*. Stono Ferry recently upgraded its greens with Bermuda grass and added a new pro shop.

Patriots Point Links – *1 Patriots Point Rd., Mt. Pleasant. 843-881-0042. www.patriotspointlinks.com*. This is golf with a view of ocean-bound cargo ships, since Charleston Harbor's shipping lanes lie just offshore.

> ### Greens Fees
>
> Greens fees in the Charleston area can run as low as $20 for a city course to over $200 for the resort courses, depending on the course, the season, the day of the week, and the time of day you play. Generally, greens fees are less expensive on weekdays and later in the afternoon. You'll often get the best deals in off-season, which in Charleston is from June to September and from December through January.

Resort Courses

You don't have to stay at Wild Dunes or Kiawah in order to play their top-notch greens, but if you're not staying at the resorts, you can't book tee times more than seven days in advance. (Off-season rates apply from December through February in the resort areas.)

Kiawah Island★★

21mi south of Charleston via Maybank Hwy. (Rte. 700) & Bohicket Rd. 843-768-2121 or 800-576-1570. www.kiawahresort.com. See The Lowcountry Coast.

Kiawah claims no less than six golf courses (the River Course is reserved for property owners), including the world-renowned Ocean Course, host to the Ryder Cup in 1991 and the World Golf Championships World Cup in 2003.

Cougar Point Golf Club – *West Beach Village.* Named for the animals that used to roam wild over the island, Cougar Point was overhauled by Gary Player in 1996.

Oak Point Golf Club – *4255 Bohicket Rd., Johns Island.* Oak Point lies just outside Kiawah's gate on a former cotton plantation.

The Ocean Course – *1000 Ocean Course Dr., on Vanderhorst Plantation. Golf Digest* rated these Pete Dye-designed oceanfront links as the country's "toughest resort course."

Osprey Point Golf Club – *Vanderhorst Plantation.* Tom Fazio fashioned Osprey Point around saltwater marshes and natural lakes.

Turtle Point Golf Club – *East Beach Village.* Rolling sand dunes edge part of Turtle Point's Jack Nicklaus design, which was updated in 2000.

Wild Dunes★

On Isle of Palms, 15mi north of Charleston via US-17 & Rte. 517. 888-778-1876. www.wilddunes.com.

Gator on the Green

Don't panic if you spot an alligator on the green; these critters are a common sight on many Lowcountry courses, especially those that border marshland (such as Kiawah and Wild Dunes). If you leave the creatures alone, they'll usually let you play through—just don't try wrestling a gator for your ball.

The private resort offers 36 holes of championship golf, in addition to its other amenities *(see The Lowcountry Coast).* Both Wild Dunes courses were designed by Tom Fazio.

Harbor Course – *5881 Palmetto Dr.* This challenging par-70 course has four holes along the Intracoastal Waterway, known to some duffers as the "world's longest water hazard."

Wild Dunes Links – *5757 Palm Blvd.* The rolling Links course is consistently ranked among "America's Top 100" courses by *Golf Magazine.*

Pack a Picnic

Surrounded on three sides by water, Charleston's peninsula has some primo places to picnic, complete with river/harbor views. When you're ready for a break from sightseeing, pack up the family, pick up some gourmet goodies, and enjoy an old-fashioned picnic.

Waterfront Park★– *On the Cooper River at the end of Vendue Range. See Parks and Gardens.* Spread a blanket on the grass or settle into one of the wooden swings on the pier at Waterfront Park, a block off bustling East Bay Street. On a hot day, little ones will enjoy frolicking in the circular fountain.

White Point Gardens★ – *Along the Battery. See Parks and Gardens.* Set at the tip of the peninsula, where the Cooper and Ashley rivers meet, White Point boasts expansive water views.

James Island County Park – *871 Riverland Dr., on James Island. 843-795-7275. www.ccprc.com/jicp.htm. See Musts for Kids.* The 643-acre county park may be a bit off the beaten track—it's across the connector on James Island—but the park comes fully equipped with covered picnic shelters.

Picnics To Go

Here are a couple of tasty places to stock up for alfresco dining:

Kennedy's Bakery and Market – *60 Calhoun St. 843-723-2026.* Owner Kevin Jordan and his staff make everything in this neighborhood artisan bakery from scratch by hand, from crusty baguettes to scrumptious cakes to gooey chocolate truffles. It's often a stop on the culinary walking tour *(see p 85)*, but, by all means, feel free to visit on your own. It's the perfect place to pick up picnic supplies, and there's a fine selection of wines under $20.

Bull Street Gourmet – *60 Bull St., at the corner of Smith St. 843-720-8992.* Bull Street's made-to-order sandwiches (the chicken salad with roasted almonds and dried cranberries gets raves), soups, deli salads, wine and imported cheeses are all available to go.

Paddle a Kayak

*Shem Creek Maritime Center, 514-B Mill St.,
Mt. Pleasant. 843-884-7684.
www.coastalexpeditions.com.*

Paddling a sea kayak silently through the area's saltmarsh creeks, you can experience the Lowcountry in a way that few people do. Coastal Expedition's three-hour naturalist-led tours *($58/person)* include basic instruction and are suited to the novice. If you're already a proficient paddler, you can rent kayaks and go off on your own *(single kayaks $38/half day, $48 full day)*. Either way, you're bound to see a multitude of marsh birds and other denizens of the tidal creeks, as well as the shrimp boats that dock at Shem Creek.

Sail the Schooner Pride

*Departs daily from Aquarium Wharf, at the
north end of Calhoun St. Schedules vary; call
or check online. 843-559-9686.
www.schoonerpride.com. $20 adults,
$15 children (ages 4-12).*

Hop aboard the 84-foot-long, 3-masted Class "C" tall ship, the *Schooner Pride*, for a look at Charleston the way the early immigrants saw it—from the decks of their sailing ships.

Resembling a 19C trading schooner, the 49-passenger vessel glides silently on its two-hour cruise. If you're feeling adventurous, the crew might just let you help trim the sails or even have a turn at the helm. *For more about harbor cruises, see Musts for Fun.*

Cooper River Bridge Run

*Registration ($20, includes T-shirt) is required for the race. 843-792-0345.
www.bridgerun.com.*

Charleston's popular 10K run draws runners from around the state. Held each April, the race starts in Mt. Pleasant and crosses the two Cooper River bridges—which are closed to vehicles for the race—to end in downtown Charleston. The 2005 event will be the last one held on the old bridge; a brand new span is slated to open by 2006 *(see p 13)*.

From the aquarium to Patriot's Point to a day at the beach, kids get a kick out of the Charleston area. Here are a few good ways to entertain the young and the restless while you're in town.

South Carolina Aquarium★★

100 Aquarium Wharf, at the east end of Calhoun St. 843-720-1990. www.scaquarium.org. Open Apr–mid-Aug Mon–Sat 9am–6pm, Sun noon–6pm. Rest of the year Mon–Sat 9am–5pm, Sun noon–5pm. Closed Thanksgiving Day & Dec 25. $15 adults; $8 children (ages 3-11). Free for children age 2 or under.

If you've ever wondered what kinds of creatures inhabit the waters around Charleston, you'll learn the answer here. From seahorses to sharks, some 7,000 creatures and 12,000 plants fill the aquarium's 60 exhibits. Opened in May 2000, the facility overlooks Charleston Harbor and the Cooper River. Exhibits focus on seven watery environments found in South Carolina, from Blue Ridge mountain streams—a habitat for playful river otters—to Coastal Plains, where black-water swamps harbor such denizens as alligators and diamondback rattlesnakes.

The Great Ocean

The aquarium's largest exhibit is two stories tall and contains more than 330,000 gallons of salt water—the water weighs as much as 457 adult African elephants! Watch 350 fish of 50 different species swim by, including a 250-pound loggerhead sea turtle, nurse sharks and porkfish, through a 28-foot-tall acrylic window. Stick around for the educational dive shows and daily fish feedings *(Mon–Sat 11am, Sun 1:30pm)*. And don't miss watching the frisky otters get their breakfast in the Mountain Forest exhibit *(Mon–Sat at 10am)*.

Just Fresh

North side of the aquarium, on the upper level of Fountain Walk in the lobby of the IMAX theater. When you're ready for lunch, here's a good place to grab freshly made sandwiches, wraps, salads and individual pizzas. Kids' meals include a choice of soft drink, chips or fruit, and a cookie. For dessert, try a cool cone or a hot cappuccino from **Wholly Cow Ice Creams! and Coffee Beans**, which shares the same space.

Touch Tank

Kids can have close encounters of the fishy kind with hermit crabs, sea urchins, horseshoe crabs and other creatures in the aquarium's Touch Tank *(on the first level)*. Staff members are on hand to answer questions and tell curious youngsters about the critters.

Riverside Terrace

Just outside the aquarium, you'll have great views of the harbor and the huge container ships that sail into the port of Charleston. If you're lucky, you might even spot some of the harbor's resident dolphins.

More Fun On Aquarium Wharf

IMAX – *Fountain Walk, upper level. 843-725-4629. www.charlestonimax.com. Open year-round daily 10am–10pm. Call for film schedules. $8.50 adult. $7.50 children (ages 3-11).* Located adjacent to the aquarium, Fountain Walk encompasses, shops, eateries and the IMAX theater. Charleston's 53-foot-high, 70mm-format IMAX screen shows a changing program of films such as *NASCAR 3D: The IMAX Experience, Coral Reef Adventure,* and *Harry Potter and the Prisoner of Azkaban.*

Harbor Cruises – S*ee Musts for Fun.* The ticket office for Spirit-Line cruises is located on the lower level of Fountain Walk.

Fort Sumter Visitor Education Center – *On the south side of the aquarium. See p 38.* Why did the North and the South pit brother against brother in 1861? Find out the answer on a boat tour to Fort Sumter, one of America's most famous forts.

Funday Sunday

Every Sunday in summer, Aquarium Wharf hosts Funday Sunday, an afternoon packed with fun for the whole family *(Jun–Aug, noon–5pm)*. Grab the kids and come on down—there'll be music, kids' crafts, face painting, mask making, jump castles and much more!

Family Fun at Middleton Place★★★

4300 Ashley River Rd. 843-556-6020. www.middletonplace.org. Open year-round daily 9am–5pm. Closed Thanksgiving Day & Dec 25. $20 adults (gardens & stableyards), $5 children (ages 7-15). Free for children under age 6.

Once a working plantation, Middleton Place *(see Plantations)* hosts a year-round schedule of events that will appeal to the whole family. Here are a couple of our favorites:

Plantation Days – *Every Saturday in Nov, 10am–4pm.* It took a lot of work to prepare a 19C plantation for harvest time. Come see for yourself in November, when craftspeople demonstrate the different aspects of plantation life, including daily tasks, traditional African-American arts and Lowcountry foodways.

Plantation Christmas – *Dec 4–31.* At Christmastime, the halls of Middleton's House Museum are decked with holly and other Yuletide finery. Tour the house, take a carriage ride, and enjoy the special holiday fare served at Middleton Place Restaurant. You might even find a few cool stocking stuffers among the handmade items sold in the museum shop.

In December, come for a special night of caroling, wreath-making and other holiday happenings at the **Family Yuletide in the Stableyards** *(call for date & times; reservations required).* The live nativity scene stars animals from the plantation's Stableyard.

Outdoor Program at Middleton Place

4300 Ashley River Rd. 843-556-6020. www.middletonplace.org. Open year-round daily 9am–5pm. Closed Thanksgiving Day & Dec 25. General admission (gardens & grounds) $20 adults; $5 children (free for children under age 6).

Since Middleton plantation embraces a varied landscape of waterways and woodlands, it's only fitting that they should share this natural wealth with visitors. Through the Middleton Place Outdoor Program, you can explore the Lowcountry via bike, kayak, on foot along interpretive nature trails, and even on horseback. Go with a guide or take off on your own—the choice is yours.

Charles Towne Landing State Historic Site

1500 Old Towne Rd. 3mi northwest of Charleston via US-17 to Rte. 171. 843-852-4200. www.southcarolinaparks.com. Open Memorial Day–Labor Day daily 8:30am–6pm. Rest of the year daily 8:30am–5pm. Closed Dec 24 & 25. $5 adults, $3 children (ages 6-15).

The site where the first group of English colonists settled in 1670 *(see Historic Sites)* also has some cool things for kids to do.

Animal Forest – Bobcats and bison and wolves—oh my! Those are just a few of the animals you'll see at this 22-acre zoo, in a natural forest setting. The catch is that all animals you'll find in the Animal Forest are the same types of critters that would have inhabited the area when the first settlers landed here.

The Adventure – *Closed for restoration until late 2005.* When it's restored, you'll be able to board the *Adventure*, a full-size replica of a 17C trading ship, docked on Old Town Creek. This is the type of ship that would have carried goods in and out of Charleston Harbor during colonial days.

Storytelling Festival

Bring the kids to this folklore festival, held at Charles Towne Landing every year in November. You'll hear fascinating tales of the early peoples, cultures and animals that roamed the area around Charleston in the decades before the first European settlers arrived. Call Charles Towne Landing for information and schedules.

Children's Museum of the Lowcountry

25 Ann St., behind the Visitor Reception Center on Meeting St. 843-853-8962. www.explorecml.com. Open year-round Tue–Sat 10am–5pm, Sun 1pm–5pm. Closed Mon & major holidays. $5/person (adults not admitted without children.)

From toddler to age ten, there's a lot of activity in store for little ones at the Children's Museum. With a mission to spark a love of learning, the museum exposes kids to the arts, sciences and humanities through a series of exhibits/play stations. Dress up as a medieval monarch in Castle Stories, create your own masterpiece with giant Lego blocks in Building Zone, or dive into art projects. Don't worry, the kids won't realize it's educational—they'll just think it's fun!

Shrimping on the Anna Marie – Here kids delight in donning boots and raincoats and running around the decks of a model shrimp boat to experience a day in the life of a Lowcountry shrimper.

Paolo's Gelato Italiano

41 John St. 843-577-0099. www.paolosgelato.com.

What better way to end a visit to the Children's Museum than to go right across the street for a creamy gelato at Paolo's? This Italian version of ice cream is made fresh daily and comes in a bunch of yummy flavors that both kids and adults will love—chocolate, carmel, strawberry, cappuccino, pina colada, Grand Marnier and more.

James Island County Park

871 Riverland Dr., on James Island. From down-town Charleston, take the James Island connector (Rte. 30) and turn right on Folly Rd. Take the next left on Central Park Rd., and left again at the stop sign onto Riverland Dr. 843-795-7275. www.ccprc.com/jicp.htm. Open May–Aug daily 8am–8pm. Rest of the year, closing times vary. $1 (free for children under age 2).

Do the kids need some space to run? This 643-acre county park should do the trick. Between picnic areas, campgrounds, ball fields, biking trails, and creeks for fishing, there's plenty of recreation here. Rent a pedal boat or a kayak, try scaling the 50-foot-high climbing wall, or let the little ones go wild at Splash Zone *(below)*. Whatever they choose, one thing's for sure: the kids won't be bored at this place.

Festival of Lights

If you're visiting Charleston around Christmastime *(mid-Nov–early Jan)*, be sure to take the family to the annual Festival of Lights, when James Island County Park creates a twinkling holiday wonderland with the help of more than 500,000 lights. The best ways to enjoy the scene: drive the 3-mile tour through the park *($10/car)*, or hop aboard the 54-passenger train *($2/person)* that tours the park.

Splash Zone

In James Island County Park. Open late May–late Aug daily 10am–6pm. May & late Aug–Labor Day weekends only 10am–6pm. $9.99 adults, $6.99 children under 42 inches tall (free for children under age 2).

Hot fun in the summertime is the focus at Splash Zone, which features a 200-foot tube slide, a 200-foot open slide, a 500-foot lazy river for tubing, and a Caribbean-themed water playground. Oh, and there's a regular pool, too (complete with lifeguards). Don't forget your bathing suit!

Must Go: Performing Arts

Think Charleston is just a place for beach parties and shoreline strolls? Think again. This coastal beacon attracts an international crowd when it comes to performing arts. With such an impressive fleet of dance, theater, and music offerings, Charleston is worth its salt as a destination for must-see productions.

Spoleto USA Festival★★

Held in various venues in Charleston, late May–mid-June. Festival information: 843-722-2764. Tickets: 843-579-3100. www.spoletousa.org. Ticket prices vary depending on performance.

Every spring, Italian flair meets southern hospitality at this renowned festival. Founded in 1977 by Pulitzer prize-winning composer Gian Carlo Menotti as the counterpart to his Festival of Two Worlds in Spoleto, Italy, the arts extravaganza showcases the best of Charleston—with its intimate size and grand spaces—as a setting for over 120 performances. Yo-Yo Ma, Emanuel Ax, the Emerson String Quartet, and Philip Glass have all appeared in years past—and the list goes on and on.

A kaleidoscope of artistic genius, the Spoleto festival includes an entire spectrum of international talent spanning opera, jazz, visual arts and multimedia presentations, to name a few. From the downtown hustle and bustle, to City Hall and throughout historic theaters and churches, Charleston offers a diverse backdrop to the festival's delights. Additional venues include the early-19C campus of the College of Charleston and the gardens of the 18C **Middleton Place★★★** plantation *(see Plantations)*. Don't miss it!

Piccolo Spoleto★

Held in various venues in Charleston, late May–mid-June. Festival information: 843-724-7305. Tickets: 843-554-6060. www.piccolospoleto.com. Ticket prices vary depending on performance.

Not only does the city welcome top productions and performers—it also generates them. As the little sister of Spoleto (*piccolo* means "small" in Italian), the Piccolo Spoleto festival presents local and regional creativity through poetry readings, ethnic cultural presentations, children's activities, choral music, and more. Highlights from previous festivals include walking tours, outdoor juried art exhibitions, public art projects (such as *Larger Than Life* featuring 15 large-scale paintings displayed on prominent Charleston buildings), music block parties, improvisational comedy by Charleston's The Have Nots! *(see Nightlife)* and many more opportunities to experience Southeastern culture. Venues range from the ridiculous (Starbucks) to the sublime (the French Huguenot Church), but the list is exhaustive and offers an excellent overview of Charleston's distinct traits.

Dock Street Theatre★

135 Church St. Box Office: 843-577-7183. www.charlestonstage.com. Box Office open 10am until curtain on show days; otherwise Mon–Fri 10am–5pm.

Concerts, operas, lectures and plays never cease to entertain in this charming historic-district venue, built as a hotel in 1809. Dock Street Theatre is home to **Charleston Stage Company** (CSC), South Carolina's largest stage troupe, which combines local talent with visiting actors from around the country to produce colorful shows like *Beneath the Sweetgrass Moon*, *Ain't Misbehavin'*, and *The Legend of Sleepy Hollow*.

Historic Dock Street Theatre, which accommodates more than 400 people, boasts a rich interior, with black-cypress wall paneling, elegant arches and the carved wood bas-relief of the Royal Arms of England. It occupies the site where an earlier Georgian-style theater once stood.

The American Theater

446 King St. www.americantheater.com. 843-853-0246.

For eclectic film buffs, here's a showstopper: dinner and a movie at the American Cinema, a renovated movie house from the Art Deco era. Designed to accommodate more than movie-watching, the theater promotes a party atmosphere in Stars Lounge, an upstairs hangout where you'll find private-label wine, desserts, and even a musician or two for live entertainment. But don't forget the box office: feature films and televised events like the Academy Awards will keep you in your seat.

The best part? Food is welcome in the theater, and your taste buds will appreciate the yummy fare offered (try a portobello burger or a chicken-pesto panini). There are even flip-up trays at each seat for simultaneous viewing and munching. At last, a feast for the eyes *and* the stomach!

Charleston Ballet Theatre

477 King St. www.charlestonballet.com. 843-723-7334.

Forget prissy tutus and prima donnas—this ballet company, founded in 1987 by artistic director Patricia Cantwell, prides itself on maintaining an energetic blend of modern and classical expression. Originally from Austria, Russia, the US, Canada, and beyond, the company's outstanding dancers form a vibrant team focused on refining and exhibiting their craft. Productions ranging from the delightful *Cinderella* to more explosive works such as *Firebird,* and *Mona Lisas and Mad Hatters*—arranged by the company's resident choreographer, Jill Eathorne-Bahr—dazzle audiences year after year.

Charleston Symphony Orchestra

843-723-7528. Tickets: www.charlestonsymphony.com.

Formed in 1918 as a loosely organized group that played mainly for friends, the Charleston Symphony Orchestra held its first formal concert in 1936 in Hibernian Hall. The professional symphony that now exists dates to 1970, when the group performed Charleston's first production of George Gershwin's folk opera *Porgy and Bess*, based on the novel by native son Dubose Heyward.

Today, a resplendent cast of musicians and guest artists (past performers include Itzhak Perlman, Pinchas Zukerman, Marvin Hamlisch and Judy Collins) fill every season *(Sept–Apr)* with sweeping sound and artistry. Led by David Stahl since 1984, CSO performs at a variety of venues, including Gaillard Auditorium *(77 Calhoun St.)* and Sottile Theatre *(opposite)*. The group, which includes 45 professional full-time musicians, brings the joy of music to the masses through a regular schedule of community concerts, school programs, and their major concert series: Masterworks, Sottile Chamber Orchestra Series, The Charleston Pops and Small Fry concerts.

North Charleston Coliseum & Performing Arts Center

5001 Coliseum Dr. Tickets: 843-554-6060 or www.ticketmaster.com. www.coliseumpac.com.

This oval arena takes on many shapes during the year: the 13,000-seat facility is home to everything from sporting events—it's the home court of the South Carolina Stingrays East Coast Hockey League team—to energetic Broadway productions such as *Fiddler on the Roof* and *Grease*, as well as performances by the Charleston Symphony Orchestra. James Taylor, Metallica, and the Ringling Bros. circus are among the acts who have made appearances here. Check out the coliseum Web site or call to get the schedule when you're in town.

Footlight Players

20 Queen St. 843-722-4487. www.footlightplayers.net.

They aren't called "footlight" for nothing—this
company has relocated more than three times
since their inception in 1931, occupying the Navy
Yard and Dock Street Theatre at different times
over the years as temporary homes. Today the
Players reside in a renovated cotton warehouse

on Queen Street,
making the most
of their long-standing tradition to deliver top-
notch performances—musicals, love stories,
dramas—to enthusiastic audiences. Productions
staged at this community theater star local
actors in such shows as *The Elephant Man*, *Little
Shop of Horrors*, and *West Side Story*.

Sottile Theatre

*44 George St., on the College of Charleston campus. 843-953-5623.
www.charlestonsymphony.com.*

When you wish upon a star, you might end up in this twinkling theater at the
College of Charleston, with its trademark saucer-shaped dome. Look above
you to marvel at the blue expanse of ceiling, accented with a sprinkling of tiny
lights; then sit back and enjoy the brilliant performances of real stars on stage.
Built in the 1920s, the theater served as an entertainment venue for films and
vaudeville productions. A meticulous structural renovation in 1986 updated
the theater's nuts and bolts, and added a spacious lobby area in front. The new
look didn't end there; they spruced up the scene behind the curtain as well,
with increased storage and dressing rooms. With all the improvements, the
Sottile continues to welcome an outstanding line-up of shows, including the
Spoleto USA Festival *(see p 100)* and the Charleston Ballet Theatre *(see p 103)*.

No wonder pirates loved this place! All the cultural delights and southern luxuries of Charleston are enough to make any treasure-seeking buccaneer weigh anchor. This seaport shopping phenomenon offers a wealth of loot, from antiques and modern art to designer labels and Lowcountry foodstuffs. What are you waiting for? Grab your gold doubloons (or green-backs) and go shopping!

Old City Market★★

On Market St. between Meeting & East Bay Sts. Open year-round daily 10am–6pm.

A three-block-long row of vendors' sheds, the historic market stretches from Meeting Street to the river along Market Street. Every morning, stalls fill with vendors peddling an array of wares, including foodstuffs, sweet grass baskets, jewelry and more.

Market Street

The blocks of Market Street adjacent to the Old City Market overflow with resort wear, fine art, souvenirs, shells and gifts.

> **Fun Fact**
>
> The first market on this site (c.1840) was a meat market. Laws at the time required vendors to sell only fresh produce; at the end of the day, merchants threw any leftover meat into the streets, where it was devoured by vultures. Known as "Charleston eagles," vultures were so important for this purpose that they were protected by law.

Scents of Charleston – *92 N. Market St. 843-853-8837.* Aromatherapy rules at this sweet-smelling shop, where you can have a fragrance customized just for you. Scents of Charleston is also the place to go for those perfumes you had trouble finding elsewhere.

Sweet Grass Baskets

As you stroll through the Old Market and along the streets in Charleston, or drive north on US-17 past Mt. Pleasant, you'll see black women making and selling a wide variety of coiled grass baskets. The coiled basketry craft came to South Carolina with slaves from West Africa 300 years ago. During the pre-Civil War plantation era, slaves winnowed rice and stored food in baskets made by coiling marsh grass with strips of palmetto leaves. In the early 20C, women began producing and selling "show baskets" made of sweet grass, a now-scarce dune grass found along the South Carolina coast. This art form, passed down from generation to generation, is now prized as a dying folk art. Labor-intensive sweet grass baskets take anywhere from 12 hours to 3 months to make, a fact that adds to their value as well as to their price.

King Street★

Charleston's major commercial thoroughfare since colonial days, King Street still brims with shops, inns and restaurants *(between Market & Broad Sts.).* Chain stores like Talbots, Victoria's Secret, Gap, and Williams Sonoma put a modern face on shopping, while connoisseurs of all things old will delight in poking through the abundant shops of the antique dealers who line the blocks of King Street between Wentworth and Queen streets.

Here's a sampling of some of King Street's more unique wares:

Charleston Place – *On the lobby level of Charleston Place Hotel, 205 Meeting St. 843-722-4900. www.charlestonplace.com.* From chain retailer to designer boutique, the mini mall in Charleston Place presents a litany of classy shops, including Walden Books, Chico's, Tommy Bahama, Godiva, Gucci, and Lacoste. For the discriminating buyer, the Venice Simplon-Orient-Express Boutique proffers an unusual (and pricey) selection of gifts.

Croghan's Jewel Box – *308 King St. 843-723-3594. www.croghansjewelbox.com.* Any Charlestonian worth his or her salt knows Croghan's. The revered family-run jeweler offers silver in all shapes and sizes in this tiny shop.

Felice Designs – *424 King St. 843-853-3354. www.felicedesigns.com.* Designer Felice Viguerie makes jewelry magic with glass beads in every possible color and combination.

Cool Shoes

King Street offers some of the coolest kicks in town. Check out **Copper Penny Shooz** *(317 King St.; 843-723-3838; www.shopcopperpenny.com)* for everything from plaid pumps to "Koolaburra" boots, and designer names from Kate Spade to Isaac Mizrahi. Can't find your dream shoe? There's no need to go over the rainbow in your search— just click your heels three times and head to **Bob Ellis** *(332 King St., 843-722-2515; www.bobellisshoes.com)* for shoes and accessories from designers around the world— think Yves Saint Laurent, Prada, Bally, and Stewart Weizeman.

Fred – *237 King St. 843-723-5699. www.fredstore.com.* A delight for gadget addicts, Fred specializes in funky and functional items for your house such as the indispensable rubber ducky, a "mr. suicide" drain stopper, silver mesh lunch boxes, and magic bunny toothpick holders. Sound crazy? We thought so, too, but Fred proves the fun is in the small stuff.

Le Creuset – *241 King St. 843-723-4191. www.lecreuset.com.* Many great cooks swear by Le Creuset's ceramic-coated cast-iron cookware. Check out the back of the store, where you can buy these French pots and pans at outlet prices.

Millennium Music – *372 King St. 843-853-1999. www.millenniummusic.com.* Music and movies, sounds and sights—it's a media extravaganza at Millennium Music.

Moo Roo – *316 King St. 843-534-2233. www.mooroo.com.* Alicia Keys, Sharon Stone, Catherine Zeta-Jones, Kim Catrall—they all have something in common, and it's not just showbiz. It's handbags! The latest buzz in Hollywood began on a kitchen table in Charleston. Inspired by a dream, designer Mary Norton let her imagination lead the way in creating unique, flamboyant purses. Her bags run the gamut from mod to magnificent: the "Brady Bunch Bouquet" is retro cool in pastel blue suede and giant flowers, while the oval-shaped "L'Opera" sparkles as a gem-studded clutch. Now the toast of Tinseltown, Moo Roo creations sell for hundreds of dollars.

Saks Fifth Avenue – *211 King St. 843-853-9888. www.saksfifthavenue.com.* Opened in 1996, this tony department store added another upscale notch to King Street's money belt.

Yves deLorme – *246 King St. 843-853-4331. www.yvesdelorme.com.* Francophiles and lovers of fine linens will drool over the luxurious sheets and towels imported by Yves deLorme. Sure, a set of sheets here might set you back a pretty penny, but you're sure to sleep like a baby on this ultra-soft cotton bedding.

Upper King Street

Once a run-down area with nary a place to eat or shop, upper King Street *(from Calhoun St. to Ann St.)* is being newly revitalized with an array of trendy options catering to those with more disposable income. Browse through furniture, clothing and specialty stores here, along with chic art galleries and restaurants featuring mouth-watering menus.

East Bay Street

Stroll around on both sides of the street, from the Old City Market to Broad Street, for trinkets and treasures. When you need a break from conspicuous consumerism, stake out a table at one of the many fine restaurants along this corridor *(see Must Eat)*.

Fine art galleries are especially plentiful along East Bay Street in the historic district. The beauty of Charleston can hardly be matched anywhere else, but at least you can take a piece of it home with you. Here are some of our favorite galleries:

American Originals – *153 E. Bay St. 843-853-5034. www.americanoriginalsgallery.com.* You'll find unique contemporary American crafts by over 350 artisans here.

Courtyard Art Gallery – *149 E. Bay St. 843-723-9172. www.courtyardartgallery.com.* This co-op features work by 14 local artists.

Eva Carter Gallery – *132 E. Bay St. 843-722-0506. www.evacartergallery.com.* Abstract art by the late William Halsey and by contemporary artist Eva Carter takes center stage at this gallery.

Gordon Wheeler Gallery – *180 E. Bay St. 843-722-2546.* Wheeler's shop showcases his limited-edition prints of golf, Lowcountry landscapes and Charleston scenes.

Waterfront Art Gallery – *215 East Bay St. 843-722-1155. www.waterfrontartgallery.com.* Charleston's largest member-owned gallery exhibits original oils, pastels, watercolors, photography and lithographic prints by 18 artists from throughout the state, including Margaret Hoybach, Joann Davis, Bob Graham and J. Michael Kennedy.

More Must-See Galleries

East Bay Street certainly doesn't have a monopoly on fine art galleries. Numerous artists, including the nationally renowned Betty Anglin Smith, exhibit their creations throughout the city, offering everything from literal renderings of the area to imaginative modern art. Here are a few galleries elsewhere in town that you shouldn't miss:

- **Charleston Renaissance Gallery** – *103 Church St. at St. Michael's Alley. 843-723-0025. www.fineartsouth.com.*
- **The Elizabeth O'Neill Verner Gallery** – *79 Church St. 843-722-4246. www.vernergallery.com.*
- **Jerald Melberg Gallery** – *8 Vendue Range. 843-965-5000. www.jeraldmelberg.com.*
- **Smith Killian Fine Art** – *9 Queen St. 843-853-0708, www.smithkillian.com.*
- **Steven Jordan Gallery** – *463 W. Coleman Blvd., Mt. Pleasant. 843-881-0788. www.stevenjordan.com.*
- **Tidwell Art Gallery** – *343 King St. 843-723-3167.*

More Must Shops

Up for more shopping? Charleston makes a career out of variety, and the area's assortment of boutiques is no exception.

Alpha Dog Omega Cat – *40 Archdale St. 843-723-1579. www.alphadogomegacat.com.* A paradise for pampered pets—and their owners. Goodies include luxury collars and leads, hand-painted home accessories, and imported trinkets.

Beachtown – *1009/1101 Ocean Blvd., Isle of Palms. 843-886-9851.* Forget to pack your swimsuit? Never fear, two Beachtown shops are near with plenty of hip attire for sun and surf.

Charleston Crafts Gallery – *87 Hassell St. 843-723-2938. www.charlestoncrafts. org.* Charleston's oldest craft co-op is a great place to buy sweet grass baskets and creations ranging from wood to glass to hand-dyed fabrics.

Clowns Bazaar – *56 Broad St. 843-723-9769.* Proceeds from sales at this tax-exempt store benefit Third-World families. Look for unique arts and crafts like carvings and silks, wooden toys, books, and, of course, clown dolls.

Historic Charleston Foundation Museum Gift Shop – *108 Meeting St. 843-724-8484. www.historiccharleston.org.* Here you'll find a good selection of books about Charleston and its history—pick up a copy of the historic district walking-tour booklet—along with some classy gifts such as ornaments and pins.

Historic Charleston Reproductions – *105 Broad St. 843-723-8292. www.historic charleston.org.* Buying non-profit products never felt so luxurious! Licensed replicas, from mahogany furniture to jewelry inspired by local iron scrollwork, fill this store with authentic souvenirs of Charleston's past.

Charleston To Go: Quintessential Souvenirs

Treasure chest still looking a little empty? That's probably because you haven't stocked up on the essentials. No trip to Charleston is complete without a sampling of classic Lowcountry plunder, so be sure to put these on your list of must-buys. They make great souvenirs for the folks back home!

Sweet grass baskets *(see p 106)* – A West African art form that's survived since the first slaves were brought to the Lowcountry, these woven wonders are hand-made in a variety of traditional and modern forms.

Moo Roo handbags *(see p 108)* – One-of-a-kind handbags with feathers, flowers, and fame are designed by local Mary Norton.

Joggling boards *(see p 23)* – Since the early 1800s, these locally made benches have offered hours of bouncy fun.

Benne seed wafers – Hit an unlucky streak? Break the spell (or at least your hunger pangs) by munching on these legendary cookies, made with the "good luck" plant (benne is the African name for sesame seeds) brought from West Africa and made famous by slave descendants in the coastal region.

Silver-plated Spoons – Even if you weren't born with a silver spoon in your mouth, you can fake it, thanks to Charleston's historic line of serving ladles. The long-handled silver utensils have been used to serve rice since the 18C. Once you've tried them, you'll agree—eating rice was never like this.

Charleston Farmers' Market

On Marion Square, at the intersection of King & Calhoun Sts. Open Mar–Dec, Sat 8am–1pm.

Be sure to stop in at this fabulous gathering of local merchants. Tomatoes from Wadmalaw Island (considered the best around), local honey, okra, figs, butter beans, peaches, grits, even wine from Charleston's only winery *(see Musts for Fun)* make this a vibrant patchwork of flavors and scents. Buy an armful of fresh flowers and take some local color with you!

The sun may slip beneath the waves on the horizon, but for those of you who shine after dark, never fear: this city isn't about to go to sleep. Whether you want to whoop it up or tone it down, Charleston's talent for combining local flavor with party flair means you'll have a good time at all hours. So put on your dancin' shoes or relax at a wine bar—whatever you do, don't miss the nightlife!

Big John's Tavern

251 E. Bay St., Historic District. 843-723-3483. www.bigjohnstavern.com.

If you're looking for a good time, you won't be disappointed by "Charleston's Best Dive Since 1955," as Big John's bills itself. Big John Canady—a former linebacker for the New York Giants—opened the tavern in 1954, never dreaming it would become a Charleston favorite. Come as a stranger and leave as a friend, as Big John advises; the convivial atmosphere means you're likely to make a new buddy while you're here. If words fail you, no worries; nightly entertainment (including dance parties and karaoke) takes the heat off so you can let your hair down.

Blind Tiger Pub

36 Broad St., Historic District. 843-577-0088. www.btpub.com.

A landmark from 1803 in Charleston's Historic District takes its name from the illegal drinking parlors opened by boisterous locals in rebellion against the Dispensary Act of 1893. Called "Blind Tigers," the parlors operated on the premise of offering "free cocktails" to patrons who came to see the legendary

(and imaginary) beast. The result? Happy drinkers and a frustrated government! Today the carousing carries on in honor of Charleston's colorful past.

Charleston Beer Works

468 King St., Historic District. 843-577-5885.

Sometimes all you need is an old standby—and that's what you'll find at the Beer Works. This popular college hangout boasts pool tables, limitless beers on tap, and $2 pints from 5pm to 8pm. Buy-one-get-one-free appetizers and occasional live music mean Happy Hour lasts into the night here.

Local Lowdown

Check the weekly *Charleston City Paper* (www.charlestoncitypaper.com) or *Preview*, the entertainment section of the *Post and Courier* (published on Thursday), for a list of what's happening when you're in town. Note that the minimum drinking age is 21 in South Carolina.

Club Habana

177 Meeting St., Historic District. 843-853-3720. www.clubhabana.com.

This upscale bar occupies the second floor of Tinderbox Internationale tobacco store. Inside the 200-year-old building, with its wood paneling, comfy couches and floor-to-ceiling windows, you can settle back and mull over the extensive drink menu—champagne, wines, martinis, single-malt scotches, small-batch bourbons, sherries, ports, madieras, imported and domestic beers. As you'd expect with a bar that's connected to a tobacco store, Club Habana is a smoking environment, but the air-filtration system here helps cut down on the smell of cigars. Stop by for Happy Hour, weekdays from 4:30pm to 7pm.

High Cotton Maverick Bar & Grill

199 E. Bay St., Historic District. 843-724-3815. www.high-cotton.net.

"High cotton" is synonymous with "livin' large," and this restaurant certainly goes the extra mile. Here, southern hospitality thrives in a sophisticated environment. Mahogany and brick create a warm, masculine setting, complemented by graceful potted palms and heart-shape straw ceiling fans. This is the place for decadent nights out. Go for live jazz on Wednesday through Friday nights.

McCrady's Wine Bar

2 Unity Alley, Historic District. 843-577-0025. www.mccradysrestaurant.com.

Part of the restaurant of the same name *(see Must Eat)*, the wine bar at McCrady's makes an intimate spot to sample that "cab" or "zin" you've been wanting to taste. Tuck into a dark booth and whisper sweet nothings to your honey while you narrow down your choice of libations from among the 30 selections of wines by the glass, taken from the restaurant's award-winning wine list. If your love doesn't fill you up, pair your favorite wine with "apps" from the small-plates menu. Ask about the schedule of wine tastings.

The Have Nots!

446 King St., at The American Theater.
843-853-6687. www.thehavenots.com.
Charleston may seem to be the epitome of etiquette, but don't be fooled. This multifaceted city holds its own in uproarious antics, too. If you want to wear yourself out with laughter, look no further than Charleston's hilarious improv troupe, along the lines of Chicago's famed Second City. The infectious energy of these quick-witted actors keeps audiences howling night after night, with interactive skits and ingenious spontaneity.

Music Farm

32 Ann St. 843-722-8904. Concert info: 843-853-3276. www.musicfarm.com.

Old MacDonald died and went to heaven: this renovated storage depot is one of the hippest barns around, but the VIPs aren't your average livestock. Instead, the spacious, multilevel scene welcomes music lovers and musicians from near and far. Tones of simplicity, from original brickwork to exposed beams, keep the focus on the music—while jazzy elements like mezzanines and a giant mural keep it fresh. The range of live music here is as wide as an open prairie. Previous performers include national acts Edwin McCain, They Might Be Giants, and Sheryl Crow, but The Farm is also known for staging the best local bands.

Vickery's Bar & Grill

15 Beaufain St., Historic District. 843-577-5300. www.vickerysbarandgrill.com.

Set in a renovated Goodyear tire store, Vickery's is a great place to meet friends for a drink on the open patio. By day, the extensive menu offers a bit of everything, including Cuban-inspired fare; at night the lively Latin ambience attracts a crowd of 20-something locals. You'll find another location in Mt. Pleasant *(1313 Shrimp Boat Lane; 843-884-4440)*, where the picturesque site takes in a view of Shem Creek and the surrounding marsh. If you arrive by boat, you can tie up at Vickery's dock before getting serious about the party scene.

Wet Willie's

209 E. Bay St., Historic District. 843-853-5650. www.wetwillies.com.

Young professionals frequent this dance club, right across from the U.S. Custom House. Thursday, Friday and Saturday nights, a DJ spins a mixed menu of dance music. If you'd rather sing yourself, go for karaoke on Sunday and Wednesday. Or you can just hang out, drink a beer and play pinball any night of the week. Wet Willie's frozen daiquiris are guaranteed to help you beat Charleston's steamy summer heat.

Zinc

28-A Bridgeside Blvd., Mt. Pleasant. 843-216-9330. www.zincbistroandbar.com.

Old World panache, good music and a swanky setting—Zinc combines all three with ease to produce a night out that's bound to impress your date. The extensive wine list—there are 80 selections by the glass—is surpassed only by the gleaming atmosphere, complete with a zinc raw bar and sushi bar. Then there's the nightly live entertainment—did we mention Big Band tunes and jazz? Relax on the canopied patio and watch the boats sail by on the Cooper River as you unwind with a glass of vino.

Beach Bars

Sure, all the church spires and historic houses are nice, but let's be honest: you came to Charleston for the beach, baby! Check out these sunny bars on **Isle of Palms★**, and don't forget to wiggle your toes in the sand.

Banana Cabana

1130 Ocean Blvd., Isle of Palms. 843-886-4361. www.diningatwatersedge.com.

If Jimmy Buffet lived in Charleston, this would be his hangout. Banana Cabana boasts a large outdoor deck with views of the ocean, a volleyball net and a putting green. A band on weekends, plus bright funky artwork make eating—and playing—here a blast. Try an outdoor Saturday lunch with lots of Bloody Marys to wash down those burgers, quesadillas and seafood.

Coconut Joe's Beach Grill and Bar

1120 Ocean Blvd., Isle of Palms. 843-886-0046. www.cocojoes.com.

Coconut Joe's beachfront upper deck is as close as you can get to the sand without being on it. This is a great spot for a seaside lunch or late-afternoon Happy Hour. There are drink specials every day, and live entertainment in season. Beat the heat with Joe's Dirty Rotten Banana, a concoction made by blending coffee liqueur, a fresh banana and vanilla ice cream. Partying into the morning? Stop by Joe's early for pina colada French toast!

The Windjammer

1008 Ocean Blvd., Isle of Palms. 843-886-8948. www.jammercam.com.

For those who can't get enough sun, sand, surf or beer, the Windjammer is for you. This is the place for bikini bashes, volleyball tournaments, bands, and, of course, beer. It's so popular that not even a hurricane can stop the crowds; after Hugo nearly demolished the original building in 1989, a new and im-proved structure appeared in its place, much to the delight of beach babes and volleyball buffs. Come out for the live bands on weekends.

The Last Resorts

While you're beaching it, don't forget Charleston's nearby island resorts: **Wild Dunes★**, just north, and **Kiawah Island★★**, to the south *(see The Lowcountry Coast)*. Both boast a beachfront bar-and-grill for quiet cocktail sipping with an ocean view.
Duney's – *At the Grand Pavilion, Wild Dunes. Open to hotel guests only.* Stroll toward the Atlantic behind the Boardwalk Inn and you'll come to Duney's. While you enjoy your beverage and drink in the views, the little ones can grab a cold one nearby at Duney's Ice Cream Shop.

Loggerhead Grill – *At The Sanctuary, Kiawah Island.* Kiawah's new luxury lodging offers several chi-chi places for a drink, but this is the only one right on the ocean *(from Memorial Day to Labor Day, the grill is only open to Sanctuary guests).*

Pounding the pavements in search of Charleston's fascinating history can be exhausting. Pamper those tired tootsies—and the rest of you—at some of the city's serene spas.

Earthling Day Spa

245 E. Bay St. 843-722-4737. www.earthlingdayspa.com.

The former Roxy Theater, a block from the Old City Market, now houses this progressive spa, whose staff blends the Indian healing techniques of Ayurveda with more traditional services. Float away into Nirvana with the package of the same name. It combines two Ayurvedic treatments: Shirodhara, where warm oils drip onto your forehead, and Bindi Herbal Bliss. In the latter, Indian herbs are used to exfoliate your skin, and warm oils are then applied to your body before sealing in the moisture under a steam canopy. Before your treatment, try out one of the Pilates classes given at the studio here.

Rick Born's Salon and Day Spa

18 Leinbach Dr., Suite G, West Ashley. 843-763-1021. www.rickbornsalon.com.

At Rick Born's you can do it all—beauty-wise, that is. Make-up, hair, nails, waxing, even airbrush tanning, are offered here. That's not to mention the spa menu of facials, body wraps and massage. The Relaxer half-day package is a good deal at $160; it includes a facial, a 75-minute massage, a shampoo and style.

Spa Adagio

387 King St., in the Westin Francis Marion Hotel. 843-577-2444. www.spaadagio.com.

"A Day at Spa Adagio" is the ultimate in pampering. Start with a sea-salt scrub, move on to a mud wrap, relax with a one-hour massage, then luxuriate with a facial, manicure and pedicure. When, at last, you're ready to leave this Historic-District spa, located in the basement of the Francis Marion Hotel, you'll feel like a new person. Aaahh.

The Spa at Charleston Place

205 Meeting St., on the 4th floor of Charleston Place Hotel. 843-937-8522.
www.charlestonplace.com.

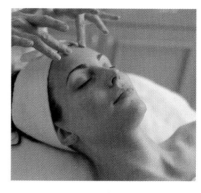

You'd expect the spa at this Orient Express property *(see Must Stay)* to be something special—and it is. The Euro-style retreat, opened in 1999, offers a full range of massage, body wraps, facials, pedicures and manicures in an atmosphere graced by imported Mexican floor tile and blond wood tones. If you want to feel like a VIP, hop into the hotel limo that takes you to and from the hotel, and treat yourself to the day-long Champagne Dreams and Caviar Wishes. You'll get a facial, French body polish, warm stone massage, lavender manicure and pedicure, and a two-hour poolside lunch—complete with Dom Perignon and Ossetra caviar, of course. Men are welcomed here with such treatments as CEO Getaway, Aqua-Man, and Groom-To-Be. The adjacent health club offers a range of fitness classes as well as a heated swimming pool, sauna and Jacuzzi. Stay for lunch and sample the spa menu—it may be low on fat, but it's high on taste. The spa has a whole list of treatments for kids as well.

Stella Nova Salon & Spa

78 Society St. 843-723-0909. www.stella-nova.com.

Just the thing while you're in the Historic District, Stella Nova sets its tony spa in a restored 19C home just off busy King Street. Stop by for an aromatherapy massage or a signature facial, or make a day of it and mix and match your choice of treatments. You might go for the 30-minute Stellar Star Glow, a body exfoliation using Dead Sea salts and pure plant oils; or Cleopatra's Secret, a 90-minute treatment that rehydrates your skin with milk and honey. For those aching feet, Pigs in Paradise includes a therapeutic soak, exfoliation and pressure-point massage, followed by a spa pedicure. There are even packages tailored to teens, as well as a three-hour "Men's Getaway." Not ready to return to reality? Sip some herbal tea and meditate in the spa's garden.

Urban Nirvana

8 Windermere Blvd. in the South Windermere shopping center, West Ashley; 843-720-8000. 636D Long Point Rd., in the Belle Hall shopping center, Mt. Pleasant; 843-881-1160. www.urbannirvana.com.

The focus is on relaxation at this suburban day spa, with locations both north and south of the peninsula. Massage specialties here encompass styles from Thai to Rain Drop (an ancient Lakota Indian healing technique using essential oils) to "Massage à Trois," with two therapists working in tandem. Smooth and hydrate your face with a customized facial, designed specifically for your skin type; or indulge in one of the body wraps, which incorporate a range of ingredients from detoxifying seaweed to invigorating coffee.

Destination Spas

When you need more than just a day of pampering, head down the coast from Charleston to these spa getaways.

The Sanctuary at Kiawah Island

1 Sanctuary Beach Dr., Kiawah Island, SC. 21mi south of Charleston via Maybank Hwy./ Rte. 700 to Bohicket Rd. 843-768-6000 or 877-683-1234. www.thesanctuary.com.

Opened in August 2004 in Kiawah's new luxury resort hotel, The Sanctuary *(see Must Stay)*, this new spa takes on the ambience of a gracious Southern porch with its potted plants, trickling waterfalls, and chaise lounges for relaxing. Natural light floods each of the 12 shuttered rooms, where such treatments as the mint julep facial and the Lowcountry verbena body polish are inspired by the area's natural features: ocean, maritime forest and lush gardens. The spa's signature Body Wraptures will melt away your stress with a massage accompanied by warm grain- and herb-filled wraps. Golfer's get their due with Golfer's Haven, a treatment that soothes those club-swinging muscles with self-heating mineral-rich sea mud, and finishes with a foot, hand and scalp massage.

Sea Island Spa

185mi south of Charleston at The Cloister, Sea Island, GA. 912-638-3611. www.cloister.com.

This renowned spa takes it treatment cues from it its Sea Island location at the tony Cloister resort. Try a Georgia mud pie wrap, an island-pine regenerative soak or perhaps a sea-spray salt glow. The 80-minute wild lime scalp and body bliss combats jet lag with a lime-oil scalp treatment followed by a full-body massage; an aroma foot wrap is sure to relieve those tired tootsies. Energy work is available, too, in the form of Reiki or craniosacral therapy. Overdone by the sun? A Sea Island sunburn soother is just what the doctor ordered!

The Spa at Palmetto Bluff

93mi south of Charleston at the Inn at Palmetto Bluff in Bluffton, SC. 476 Mt. Pelia Rd., Bluffton, SC. 843-706-6500. www.palmettobluffresort.com.

Set amid bright gardens, old forests and lazy rivers, Palmetto Bluff makes a perfect place to luxuriate. This new resort and spa is the newest in the line of upscale Auberge properties—as in Auberge du Soleil in California's Napa Valley. Sit back and enjoy a cocktail here—a bath cocktail, that is. You're sure to find the formula that is just right for you among the infusions of aphrodisiac oils (for that bath *à deux*), detoxifying cypress and juniper, or stress-relieving lemon balm and jasmine. Of course, there's a full menu of massages, exfoliations, wraps and facials. Spa packages cater to everyone from Southern belles to avid golfers.

The Grand Strand ★★

Fun is the order of the day here. A 60-mile line of beachfront, the Grand Strand marches up the coast of South Carolina along US-17 from George-town *(60mi north of Charleston)* to Little River. Sandwiched by the Intra-coastal Waterway on the west and the Atlantic Ocean on the east, the Grand Strand's nerve center is Myrtle Beach. To the south lie the low-key coastal communities of Surfside Beach, Murrells Inlet (a great place for fresh seafood), Litchfield Beach and Pawleys Island. In addition to the lure of the sand and surf, the area draws duffers from all over the country to its 120 championship golf courses.

The sights in this section are organized from north to south, beginning with Myrtle Beach.

Myrtle Beach ★

98mi north of Charleston on US-17. Visitor information: 843-626-7444. www.myrtlebeachinfo.com. Visitor centers are located at: 1200 N. Oak St. and at 1800 US-501 West, near the intersection of Rte. 22 (for visitor center hours and more practical information, see p 122).

The pulsing playground that is Myrtle Beach booms nearly year-round with people, traffic, and more entertainment options than you could possibly find time to do. But it wasn't always this way. Before 1900, this part of the coast was a quiet backwater. Enter the Burroughs & Collins Company, a turpentine manufacturer who built the first hotel on the beach in 1901. The wife of the company's founder named the area Myrtle Beach, for the abundance of wax myrtle trees that grew wild along the shore.

After Hurricane Hazel razed the Grand Strand in 1954, the rebuilding boom included something new—golf courses. Throughout the 1970s and 80s, residential and com-mercial projects mushroomed, resulting in the megaresort you see here today—one of the fastest-growing areas in the country.

Tribute! The Concert

MYRTLE BEACH

Alabama Theatre
46th Ave. S.
48th Ave. S.
Barefoot Landing
Alligator Adventure
North Gate Rd.
Briarcliffe Acres
Middle Gate Rd.

Conway

Barefoot Resort & Golf

Colonial Mall
Tanger Outlet Center
Hilton

Arcadian Shores Golf Club
Lake Arrowhead

Waterway Hills Golf Club

Lake Arrowhead Rd.

Hotels
1. Anderson Inn
2. Beach Colony Resort
3. The Breakers Resort Hotel
4. Hampton Inn, Broadway at the Beach
5. Ocean Creek Plantation Resort

Restaurants
1. Collector's Cafe
2. Croissants Bakery & Cafe
3. Hard Rock Cafe
4. House of Blues
5. The Library
6. Phillips Seafood
7. Sea Captain's House

Dixie Stampede

The Dunes Golf & Beach Club

Carolina Opry

62nd Ave. N.

79th Ave. N.

67th Ave. N.

62nd Ave. N.

ATLANTIC

THE GRAND

OCEAN

Pine Lakes Intl. Country Club

48th Ave. N.

Myrtlewood Golf Club

44th Ave. N.

38th Ave. N.

International World Tour Golf Links

29th Ave. N.

Ripley's Aquarium

Myrtle Square Mall

Broadway at the Beach

Myrtle Beach Convention Center

NASCAR SpeedPark

21st Ave. N.

Myrtle Waves Water Park

10th Ave. N.

City Hall

Myrtle Beach Pavilion & Amusement Park

River Oaks Golf Plantation

Coastal Grand

3rd Ave. S.

Family Kingdom Amusement & Waterpark

Waccamaw Factory Shoppes

Pine Island Rd.

5th Ave. S.

Fantasy Harbour

Medieval Times

9th Ave. S.

17th Ave. S.

Arrowhead Country Club

Harrelson Blvd.

Whispering Pines Golf Course

21st Ave. S.
25th Ave. S.

MYRTLE BEACH INTERNATIONAL

29th Ave. S.

STRAND

Springmaid Beach

Myrtle Beach State Park ★

MYRTLE BEACH

MYRTLE BEACH PRACTICAL INFORMATION

Visitor Information – Stop for information and maps at one of the following visitor centers:

Myrtle Beach Area Chamber of Commerce

1200 N. Oak St.; 843-626-7444
www.myrtlebeachinfo.com
Open Mar–Labor Day Mon–Fri 8:30am–5pm, weekends 9am–5pm. Rest of the year weekend hours are limited to 9am–noon.

Myrtle Beach/Grand Strand Welcome Center

1800 US-501 West, near Rte. 22; 843-626-7444
www.myrtlebeachinfo.com
Open Mar–Labor Day daily 8:30am–6pm. Rest of the year daily 8:30am–5pm.

Swimming Safely

Be sure to pay attention to beach safety flags posted on the beach: yellow means there's a lifeguard on duty; blue means it's dangerous to swim; red means no swimming allowed.

Always swim with a buddy. If you encounter a **riptide**—a strong current that can sweep you out to sea as fast as 3- to 6mph—don't try to fight it. Immediately yell for help. If help doesn't come right away, stay relaxed and swim parallel to the shore until you are free from the current's pull.

When To Go – Unlike in Charleston, high season in Myrtle Beach is in the summer—despite the searing heat. In off-season (late fall and winter), the weather is often mild, and you can get deep discounts on beachfront hotels.

Getting There – **Myrtle Beach International Airport (MYR)** is located south of 17th Avenue off Highway 15 *(1100 Jetport Rd.; 843-448-1589; www.flymyrtlebeach.com).* The airport is served by Air Canada, Continental, US Airways, Delta Connection, ComAir and Spirit, as well as Hooter's Air. Major rental-car companies have facilities at the airport.

Myrtle Beach lies roughly halfway between New York City and Miami, Florida, within an hour's drive of I-95, I-20, I-26 and I-40.

Driving in Myrtle Beach – The Grand Strand's commercial strip, Business 17, can be a frustrating place to navigate, especially in the summer season when families flock here in droves and the road, with its many traffic lights, seems more like a parking lot (Myrtle's most crowded period is 4th of July week).

All of Myrtle's major arteries parallel the Atlantic Ocean. Here's the lowdown on the main beach roads:

Ocean Boulevard (Rte. 73) runs right along the Atlantic from Myrtle Beach State Park to 79th Avenue North.

Kings Highway, aka Business 17, is the next road to the west. This often-congested thoroughfare branches off US-17 in Murrells Inlet and reconnects with it north of 79th Avenue.

US-17 Bypass is the route to take if you want to bypass the main drag.

The Grand Strand

Accommodations – *For a listing of specific hotels, see Must Stay.* While there is no lack of hotels and motels in Myrtle Beach, if you plan to stay for a week or more, or if you're traveling with a large family or a group of families, renting a condominium or vacation villa may be the most economical way to go. For a free guide to the Grand Strand, including an extensive listing of available real-estate rentals, contact the Myrtle Beach Area Chamber of Commerce *(opposite)*. When you book your lodging, be sure to ask about golf or other special package deals.

On The Beach – Lifeguards are on duty on most Grand Strand beaches during the summer months. Swimming is not permitted beyond 50 yards from the beach, or if water is over your shoulder height.

Here are some more rules and regulations:
- Glass containers and open containers of any alcoholic beverage are not permitted on the beach.
- It's illegal to drive on the beach or to set off fireworks.
- Thong bathing suits are outlawed on Myrtle's public beaches.
- It's against the law to cut, break or destroy sea oats, beach grass or sand fencing.

Dogs on the Beach

In Myrtle Beach, no animals are allowed on the beach or on Ocean Boulevard from 13th Avenue South to 21st Avenue North at any time of the year. From mid-May to mid-September, dogs are allowed on the beach only before 9am and after 5pm. Dogs must be leashed at all times in public. Pet owners are responsible for picking up after their pups.

Family Fun

Think how disappointed the kids would be if you went to Myrtle Beach and didn't sample some of its many amusement parks. Here are a few of our favorites:

Alligator Adventure – *4898 US-17, at Barefoot Landing, North Myrtle Beach. 843-361-0789. www.alligatoradventure.com. Open year-round daily. Hours vary seasonally; call or check online for schedule. $13.95 adults, $8.95 children (ages 4-12).*

If you haven't come across any alligators in your Lowcountry wanderings, you're sure to see some here—more than 800 of them, in fact. Along with garden variety and albino gators, you'll see snakes, tortoises, and the gargantuan Utan, "King of Crocs"—measuring 20 feet long and weighing in at more than 2,000 pounds.

Myrtle Beach Pavilion – *Ocean Blvd. at 9th Ave. N. 843-913-5200. www.mbpavilion.com. Hours vary seasonally; call or check online for schedule. All-day ride pass $23.95 adults, $14.88 children (ages 3-6).* Built in 1949, this 11-acre amusement park is a classic Myrtle Beach attraction. Forty rides and numerous skill games, including an oceanfront arcade, spell fun for the whole family here. Ride the 110-foot-high Hurricane Category 5 wooden roller coaster—if you dare. Not so brave? Try the Mad Mouse, the Log Flume, or, if you're a real weenie, go for the old-fashioned carousel.

Myrtle Waves Water Park – *Hwy. 17 Bypass & 10th Ave. N. 843-448-1026. www.myrtlewaves.com. Open mid-May–mid-Sept. Hours vary seasonally; call or check online for schedule. $23.95 adults, $14.95 children (ages 3-6).*

Beat the summer heat at this 20-acre water park, where you can tube down a lazy river, play in the surf at the Ocean in Motion wave pool, or rocket down the dark Turbo Twister tube slides at 50mph. The 32 water rides here include tamer Bubble Bay for toddlers.

NASCAR SpeedPark – *US-17 Bypass & 21st Ave. N. 843-918-8725. www.nascarspeedpark.com. Open year-round daily. Hours vary seasonally; call or check online for schedule. Closed Thanksgiving Day & Dec 25. $24.95 adults, $14.95 children (ages 12 and under).*

South Carolinians love their NASCAR, as you'll see at this 26-acre amusement park—an official property of the National Association for Stock Car Auto Racing. The seven racetracks here range from the half-mile Thunder Road course *(you must be 64 inches tall, at least 16 years old, and have a valid driver's license for this one)* to the 200-foot Qualifier starter track for kids *(riders must be at least 40 inches tall)*. Oh, and of course, there's mini golf, too.

Planet Hollywood

2915 Hollywood Dr., across from Broadway at the Beach (US-17 Bypass & 29th Ave. N.). 843-448-7827. www.planethollywood.com.

If you're a film buff, you've got to visit this blue-green sphere, if only to see the décor. Every nook and cranny is crammed with movie memorabilia. The food centers on family-pleasing fare: salads, sandwiches, steaks, burgers and pasta. Kids will like the Chicken Crunch, strips of chicken sugar-coated with Cap'N Crunch™ cereal. Be sure to take home a souvenir T-shirt.

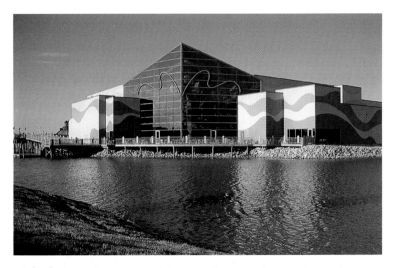

Ripley's Aquarium – *1110 Celebrity Circle, at Broadway at the Beach. 843-916-0888. www.ripleysaquarium.com. Open year-round daily 9am–11pm. $16.95 adults, $9.95 youth (ages 9-11), $3.95 children (ages 2-4).* Toothy tiger sharks, Goliath groupers, and bright green moray eels are just a few of the denizens that inhabit this 87,000-square-foot facility. Take a walk through the **Dangerous Reef**, where you'll be surrounded by 750,000 gallons of salt water and a host of sea creatures from sharks to sea turtles. You can meet some of the aquarium's critters up close at Discovery Center touch pool and at Friendship Flats, where you can pet a stingray. Stick around for the daily dive shows *(check at admission desk for schedule).*

Carolina Safari Jeep Tours

Departs from Myrtle Beach area hotels and resorts year-round daily (call for schedule). 843-272-1177. www.carolinasafari.com. $30 adults, $15 children (ages 12 & under). Ready to see some species other than *homo sapiens*? Climb aboard these covered custom jeeps for a look at the wilder side of Myrtle Beach. The naturally wild side, that is. During the 3^1/$_2$-hour excursion, you'll visit a Waccamaw Neck oyster bed, an uninhabited barrier island, and several historic sites, including the haunted churchyard where American poet James Dickey lies buried.

Entertainment

From rootin' tootin' stampedes to country-music concerts, Myrtle Beach really knows how to put on a show. And most of it's family friendly, too. Y'all come!

Alabama Theatre – *4898 US-17, at Barefoot Landing, North Myrtle Beach. 843-272-1111. www.alabama-theatre.com. Shows at 7:30pm. Call or check online for concert schedule.* Opened in 1991, thanks to a collaboration between the country-music group Alabama and Gaylord Entertainment, the Alabama Theatre presents a regular schedule of concerts (think Loretta Lynn, Roy Clark, The Drifters) in addition to its signature musical and dance extravaganza, **One**, which premiered in 2004.

Carolina Opry – *US-17 Bypass at N. Kings Hwy. 843-913-4000. www.carolinaopry.com. Call or check online for concert schedule. No shows Sun. $31.95 adults, $15 children (ages 3-16).* The 2,200-seat Carolina Opry presents music, dance and comedy. From rock 'n roll to Gospel to country classics, this two-hour variety show will keep your toes tapping. It's consistently rated one of the best at the beach.

Dixie Stampede – *8901-B US-17, North Myrtle Beach. 843-497-9700. www.dixiestampede.com. Hours & times vary seasonally; call or check online for schedule. $35.99 adults, $18.99 children (ages 4-11).* The South shall rise again . . . or will it be the North? You be the judge at this rousing competition, complete with music, dancing, horses, beefy buffaloes and a generous Southern dinner.

Medieval Times – *2904 Fantasy Way, off Rte. 501 at Fantasy Harbour. 843-236-2611. www.medievaltimes.com. Hours & times vary seasonally; call or check online for schedule. $44.02 adults, $25.75 children (ages 12 & under).* Here's another dinner show, only this one's a  joust. Watch gallant knights on horseback battle for their honor—and the love of a beautiful princess, of course. Kids will love eating with their hands, just the way folks did it in medieval times.

Tribute! The Concert – *701 Main St., North Myrtle Beach. 843-913-4444. www.tributetheconcert.com. Call or check online for concert schedule. $19.95–$28.95 adults, $14 children (ages 3-16).* New in 2004, this show stars some of the country's top tribute artists impersonating the likes of Cher, Little Richard, Frank Sinatra and Elvis. The line-up changes regularly.

Doing the Shag

If you go nightclubbing while you're in town, you're bound to encounter the shag. Born on Ocean Drive in Myrtle Beach in the mid-20C, the shag is South Carolina's signature dance. The four-count steps, which resemble the swing to the uninitiated, are performed to the tune of 120-beat-per-minute "beach music"—not to be confused with the more widely known sounds that came out of California in the 1960s. South Carolina beach music (by such groups as The Drifters and The Coasters) embodies the rhythm-and-blues tunes of the 1950s that grew up along the coast here. So grab your khakis and loafers—no socks!—and remember to keep your feet moving and your upper body relatively still. Before you know it, you'll be shagging, too.

The Grand Strand

Golf

Some 4.2 million rounds of golf are played in the Myrtle Beach area each year on 120 courses. While they're way too numerous to list all of them here, the following list will whet your golf appetite. *For a complete menu of courses, check online at: www.myrtlebeachgolf.com.*

Arrowhead Country Club – *1201 Burcale Rd., Myrtle Beach. 843-236-3243. www.arrowheadcc.com.* Three separate 9-hole tracts here border the Intracoastal Waterway.

Greens Fees

Greens fees in Myrtle Beach can run as low as $40 to over $200, depending on the course, the season, the day, and the time you play. Generally, greens fees are less expensive on weekdays and later in the afternoon. You'll often get the best deals in off-season, which in the resort area is from mid-November through February.

Barefoot Resort & Golf – *4980 Barefoot Resort Bridge Rd., North Myrtle Beach. 843-390-7900. www.barefootgolf.com.* Choose among the four courses here according to your favorite designer: Tom Fazio, Pete Dye, Davis Love or Greg Norman.

Blackmoor – *6100 Longwood Rd., Murrells Inlet. 843-650-5555. www.blackmoor.com.* Lowcountry beauty abounds at Blackmoor, built on the grounds of an antebellum rice plantation along the Waccamaw River.

Caledonia Golf & Fish Club – *369 Caledonia Dr., Pawleys Island. 843-237-3675. www.fishclub.com.* Caledonia is consistently rated among the country's top public courses in the golf press.

The Dunes Golf & Beach Club – *9000 N. Ocean Blvd., Myrtle Beach. 843-449-5914. www.dunesgolfandbeachclub.com.* Built in 1948, this popular Robert Trent Jones course was the second one to open in the area.

International World Tour Golf Links – *2000 World Tour Blvd., Myrtle Beach. 843-236-2000. www.worldtourmb.com.* Playing World Tour's 27 holes is your passport to some of the world's best-known golf layouts.

Litchfield Country Club – *US-17 South, Pawleys Island. 843-235-6079. www.primetimesgolf.com.* Live oaks and Southern pines form the backdrop for this Willard Byrd course.

Man O' War – *5601 Leeshire Blvd., Myrtle Beach. 843-236-8000. www.mysticalgolf.com.* Golf architect Don Maples created the challenging par-72 layout around an 80-acre lake.

Possom Trot Club – *1170 Possom Trot Rd., North Myrtle Beach. 843-272-5341. www.possomtrot.com.* Reasonable rates and a helpful staff are the benchmarks of this club.

Tidewater Golf Club & Plantation – *1400 Tidewater Dr., North Myrtle Beach. 800-446-5363. www.tide-water.com.* Often compared to the famed Pebble Beach Links, Tidewater sits high on a bluff overlooking the Intracoastal Waterway.

Mini Golf

Sure, you'll get your time on the links, but what about the kids? With 50 mini-golf courses in the Myrtle Beach area, you'll be hard-pressed to avoid them, no matter where you go. Pick a theme, from prehistoric dinosaurs to pirate ships to erupting volcanoes. Just don't be surprised if the kids score lower than you do! *For a list of area courses, check online at www.myrtlebeachinfo.com.*

Shopping

Don't wait for a rainy day to check out the numerous shopping malls and more than 300 outlet stores in Myrtle Beach. Go ahead, try these out for size:

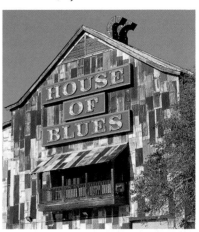

Barefoot Landing – *4898 US-17, North Myrtle Beach (adjacent to Barefoot Resort). 843-272-8349. www.bflanding.com. Open year-round daily. Hours vary by season.* Talk about all-inclusive entertainment—Barefoot Landing holds Alligator Adventure *(see p 124)*, the House of Blues *(opposite)*, and Alabama Theatre *(see p 127)*, not to mention 100 specialty shops, a handful of factory outlets, and more than a dozen restaurants. Set around a 27-acre lake, it's all made to look weathered, like an old-fashioned fishing village.

Outlet Shopping

Looking for bargains? You'll find them in spades along the Grand Strand. *The outlets mentioned below have extended hours in summer.*

Tanger Outlet Centers – *US-17 at Hwy. 22; 843-449-0491. Open year-round Mon–Sat 9am–10pm, Sun 10am–7pm. Second location on Hwy. 501, 3mi west of the Intracoastal Waterway; 843-236-5100, ext. 107. www.tangeroutlet.com. Open year-round Mon–Sat 9am–9pm, Sun 11am–7pm. Both centers are closed Easter Sunday, Thanksgiving Day & Dec 25.* Between its two locations, Tanger offers some 175 outlet stores. From Adidas shoes to Zales jewelry, you'll find a veritable ABCs of discounts here, encompassing designer clothing, cookware, cosmetics, toys and much, much more.

Waccamaw Factory Shoppes – *Hwy. 501 at the Intracoastal Waterway. 843-236-6152. www.waccamawfactoryshoppes.com. Open year-round Mon–Sat 9am–7pm, Sun 10am–6pm.* This is the original outlet mall in Myrtle Beach. The highlight here is the Waccamaw Pottery, housing everything imaginable in the way of housewares, linens and garden décor.

Broadway at the Beach – *US-17 Bypass at 21st Ave. N. 843-444-3200. www.broadwayatthebeach.com. Open year-round daily; hours vary by season. Closed Dec 25.* You never have to leave this lakeside complex, unless you want to go to the beach. Hotels, nightclubs, movie theaters, and attractions from Ripley's Aquarium *(see p 126)* to a carousel park for the wee ones—you'll find it all here. Then there's 11 nightclubs—think Club Boca, for lovers of Latin dance, and Revolutions Dance Club for you disco hounds—and 20 restaurants, including the Hard Rock Café and Jimmy Buffet's Margaritaville. All this, plus 100 shops and, of course, mini golf. Oh, and did we mention Myrtle Waves and NASCAR SpeedPark are just across the street *(see p 125)*.

Coastal Grand – *US-17 Bypass at Hwy. 501. 843-839-9100. www.coastalgrand.com. Open year-round Mon–Sat 10am–9pm, Sun noon–6pm.* Opened in March 2004, the area's biggest enclosed mall features Southern department-store anchors Belk and Dillard. Ambercrombie & Fitch, Ann Taylor Loft, Tropical Shades and Swim 'N Sport number among the 100 other stores at Coastal Grand.

House of Blues

4640 US-17 at Barefoot Landing, North Myrtle Beach. 843-272-3000. www.hob.com. This shabby-chic music venue/restaurant may appear to be a big weathered barn, but looks are deceiving. Opened in Myrtle Beach in 1997, HOB (as they call themselves) features a year-round schedule of rock and blues bands, such as Charlie Daniels, the Atlanta Rhythm Section, and Catfish Lane. Oh, and don't forget the food. You'll see definite New Orleans accents in the generous portions of Creole seafood jambalaya, Cajun meatloaf, seared voodoo shrimp, and crispy catfish nuggets with sweet-potato shoestring fries. Set your toes to tapping at the Sunday Gospel brunch—it's fun for the whole family!

The Grand Strand

Myrtle Beach State Park★

4mi south of Myrtle Beach on US Business 17. 843-238-5325.
www.discoversouthcarolina.com/stateparks. Open year-round daily dawn–dusk. $3.

Here's a beach at Myrtle without the backdrop of high-rise hotels and amusement parks. Developed by the Civilian Conservation Corps in the 1930s, the pretty 312-acre state park preserves a one-mile stretch of beachfront as well as one of the last stands of maritime forest on this part of the South Carolina coast.

Pawleys Island

Colonial rice planters had the right idea. They began coming to Pawleys Island in the 19C to escape their mosquito-infested plantations. Today shabby-chic Pawleys Island and its next-door neighbor, **Litchfield Beach**, cater to families who rent houses along this four-mile stretch of sand on the east side of the Waccamaw River. With none of the high-rise hotels, amusement parks and other hoopla associated with nearby Myrtle Beach, quiet Pawleys enjoys a laid-back ambience. There are no blaring radios, no beach volleyball, no noisy jet skis—just quiet sunning, swimming and strolling.

Touring Tip

Although Pawleys Island claims some of the prettiest beaches on the Grand Strand, it's difficult to access them if you're not staying here. Most of the land is private and public beach-access points are rare.

The Humble Hammock

What do you do when the grass-filled mattresses on your river-boat prove too hot and uncomfortable during the humid summers in the Lowcountry? You invent a rope bed. At least, that's what Captain Joshua John Ward did in the late 1800s. Ward, who transported supplies to the large rice plantations around Georgetown, South Carolina, came up with the idea of making a hanging bed of rope, to allow for greater air circulation. And it was portable, to boot. For more than one hundred years, his invention has remained unaltered; it still serves as the design for the Pawleys Island hammocks sold at the Original Hammock Shop today *(see below)*. Take one home for those alfresco naps!

Hammock Shops Village – *10880 Ocean Hwy. (US-17), Pawleys Island. 843-237-8448. Shops open Mon–Sat 10am–6pm, Sun 1pm–5pm.* Fronting this collection of 25 stores and eateries, all connected by dirt paths beneath tall pines, the **Original Hammock Shop** *(843-237-9122; www.thehammockshop.com)* —a Pawleys Island staple since the 1930s—occupies a Lowcountry-style cottage. Attached to it, the **Hammock Shop General Store** stocks beach clothes, books, bath products, birdhouses and other wares; don't leave without sampling a piece of the store's famous fudge. In the adjacent shed, artisans craft the famous Pawleys Island's rope hammocks, handwoven since 1889 *(see sidebar above)*. At the far end of the strip, **Christopher and Eve** specializes in high-quality, high-priced women's wear. In between, you'll find more clothiers for women, children and pets; a women's shoe store; a Christmas shop; art galleries; gift shops; a gourmet deli; and two restaurants—including **Louis's at Pawleys** *(see Must Eat)*.

Brookgreen Gardens★★

3mi south of Pawleys Island off US-17. 1931 Brookgreen Dr., in Murrells Inlet. 843-235-6000. www.brookgreen.org. Open year-round daily 9:30am–5pm. Closed Dec 25. $12 adults, $10 youth (ages 13-18).

Art and nature combine to form a stunning landscaped setting here. Opened in 1932 as America's first sculpture garden, Brookgreen is the love-child of artist **Anna Hyatt Huntington** and her husband, Archer, who created the gardens on the 900-acre grounds of an antebellum rice plantation.

Touring Tip

Admission tickets to Brookgreen are good for seven consecutive days. Daily garden walks, tours and special programs—not including creek cruises—are included in the admission fee. And if you have little ones in tow, children age 12 and under are admitted free when accompanied by an adult. A tram runs regularly, transporting visitors to three different points in the gardens, including the full-service restaurant and snack bar on the grounds. You could easily spend a half-day here.

Huntington Sculpture Garden – This 30-acre display garden forms Brookgreen's centerpiece. Here, major sculptures anchor individual garden "rooms," serving as focal points at the end of long walkways. The noted sculpture collection, most of which is displayed outside in the gardens, contains more than 800 works of **American sculpture** (early 19C to present) by the likes of Daniel Chester French, Augustus St. Gaudens, Paul Manship, and Anna Hyatt Huntington herself.

Lowcountry History and Wildlife Preserve – The last stop on the tram, the Lowcountry Trail loops through the woods past enclosures where bald eagles, great horned owls, foxes, and other native critters are displayed. Many of these animals found a home at Brookgreen because they were injured and are unable to live on their own in the wild. For a closer look at the wildlife preserve, catch one of the creek cruises *(see sidebar below)*.

Creek Cruises

One-hour cruises depart from the boat dock at the Lowcountry center, daily 11am, 1pm, 2pm & 3pm. $7 adults, $4 children (ages 12 & under). Evening cruises available in summer (mid-Jun–mid-Aug Wed–Fri, 5:30pm & 6:30pm). Bring binoculars and mosquito repellant. Kids and adults alike will enjoy a ride on Brookgreen's 48-passenger pontoon boat, which travels deep inside the preserve through black-water creeks once used to irrigate rice fields. Now, instead of rice paddies, the wetlands are home to alligators, snakes, hawks, osprey, and a host of other creatures. Along the way, your guide will tell you about the labors involved in cultivating and harvesting the rice known as Carolina Gold *(see p 60)*.

Huntington Beach State Park ★

Across from Brookgreen Gardens on the east side of US-17. 16148 Ocean Hwy., Murrells Inlet. 843-237-4440. www.discoversouthcarolina.com/stateparks. Open Apr–late Oct daily 6am–10pm. Rest of the year Sat–Thu 6am–6pm, Fri 6am–8pm. $5.

Want an escape from the high-rise hotels and crowds at Myrtle Beach? Huntington Beach is the place. Huntington's 3 miles of breathtakingly beautiful unspoiled beach is a destination in itself, not to mention the acres of salt marshes, where more than 300 species of birds have been spotted.

Besides the beach, the park is home to **Atalaya**, the winter residence of Anna Hyatt and Archer Huntington, who founded Brookgreen Gardens *(p 134)*. You can tour the Moorish-style castle in summer *(visit by 1-hour guided tour only, Jun–Aug Tue–Sat 2pm)*. There's plenty of camping here, and nature lovers may discover the diverse wildlife of the park's marshland ecosystem either on their own along the site's trails, or through the various land and water tours offered through the Coastal Exploration program *(summer only; call or check online for schedule)*.

Hopsewee Plantation

30mi south of Brookgreen Gardens off US-17. 494 Hopsewee Rd., Georgetown. 843-546-7891. www.hopsewee.com. Visit by 30-minute guided tour only, Mar–Oct Mon–Fri 9:30am–4:30pm. Rest of the year Thu & Fri 9:30am–4:30pm. Closed weekends & major holidays. $10. Grounds only, $5/vehicle.

Set on the Santee River, this Lowcountry indigo plantation is remarkable as the birthplace of Thomas Lynch Jr., who at age 26 was the youngest legislator to sign the Declaration of Independence. Lynch and his father, Thomas Sr., were the only father-and-son team to serve as members of the nation's Continental Congress. Made of black cypress, the two-story Georgian home (1740), with its steep hipped roof and graceful double piazza (added in 1846), is now privately owned. Inside, you'll see fine examples of 18C and 19C American and European furnishings.

Traveling for Health?

In 1776 the junior Thomas Lynch retired from political life due to health problems. After living at nearby Peachtree Plantation for three years, Lynch and his wife, Elizabeth, decided to take a trip to Europe, hoping that a change of climate would improve his failing health. In a cruel twist of fate, their ship was lost at sea on the out-going voyage; none of the passengers survived.

South Carolina Treat: Boiled Peanuts

As you drive along US-17 through some of the little towns, you're likely to see signs advertising "boiled peanuts." Sold at tiny off-road stands, this odd-sounding food is considered a treat by many native South Carolinians. After being boiled in brine in their shells, the nuts are soft and salty. Many people think boiled peanuts are an acquired taste; try some and decide for yourself.

Hampton Plantation State Park

16mi southwest of Georgetown off US-17. 1950 Rutledge Rd., McClellanville. 843-546-9361. www.discoversouthcarolina.com/stateparks. Visit of house by 1-hour guided tour only, Memorial Day–Labor Day daily 11am–4pm. Rest of the year Thu–Mon 1pm–4pm. Closed Tue, Wed & Dec 25. $4.

A French Huguenot family named Horry established this rice plantation in the mid-18C. Today the 337-acre Lowcountry estate showcases the elegant white Georgian-style mansion that began as a six-room farmhouse in 1750. You'll recognize the house by its columned two-story portico, added in 1791 by Daniel Huger Horry. Horry's mother-in-law, Eliza Lucas Pinckney *(see sidebar below),* brought the design back from England.

> **Touring Tip**
>
> With its picnic grounds and its lovely wooded setting in Francis Marion National Forest, Hampton Plantation makes a great place for an alfresco lunch. Admission to the grounds is free *(open Memorial Day–Labor Day daily 9am–6pm; rest of the year Thu–Mon 9am–6pm).*

(Eliza made her final home at Hampton with her daughter, Harriott.) The last of the family line to occupy the residence was Archibald Rutledge, Poet Laureate of South Carolina, who died here in 1973. The house remains unfurnished, and unrestored in places, in order to illustrate the original building techniques, such as the timber framing with its mortise-and-tenon joints, used to construct the home.

The Original Indigo Girl

Born to a British Army officer stationed in Antigua, Eliza Lucas (1722–1793) was 16 when her father, Lt. Col. George Lucas, moved the family to a plantation in South Carolina. The same year, Lucas was recalled to his post in Antigua, leaving his teenage daughter to run the plantation. And run it, she did. After her father sent her some indigo seeds from the West Indies, the young girl spent three years trying to cultivate the plant and learning how to extract the deep-blue dye—in great demand in England for military uniforms. Thanks to Eliza's successful experiments, Charleston's export of indigo mushroomed from 5,000 pounds in 1746 to 130,000 pounds two years later.

In 1744 Eliza married widower Charles Pinckney and assumed the management of several of her husband's estates. Their sons, Charles Cotesworth *(see Plantations/Boone Hall)* and Thomas, both distinguished themselves in early-American politics. When she died in 1793, **Eliza Lucas Pinckney** was so revered that President George Washington insisted on being one of the pallbearers at her funeral.

The Lowcountry Coast★

Named for the soggy coastal prairies that line the low-lying South Carolina coast north and south of Charleston, the Lowcountry incorporates quaint towns and a unique geography marked by acres upon acres of water-laced marshes. Here you'll discover a host of wildlife along with a range of attractions from Gullah heritage sites to the upscale resort islands of Isle of Palms, Kiawah and Hilton Head. Whether it's peace and quiet or action you seek, you'll find it along the Lowcountry Coast.

See maps pp 48–49 and on inside back cover. Sights in this section are arranged in geographical order, from north to south, beginning with Isle of Palms.

Wild Dunes★

15mi north of Charleston on Isle of Palms. Take US-17 North to the Isle of Palms Connector (Rte. 517). When the connector ends at Palm Blvd., go left at the light and follow Palm Blvd. After Palm Blvd. jogs left at 41st Ave., take the first right (continuation of Palm Blvd.). Turn left across from 48th Ave. at the gate for Wild Dunes. 888-778-1876. www.wilddunes.com.

Bounded by the Intracoastal Waterway on one side and the Atlantic Ocean on the other, Wild Dunes sprawls out over acres of salt marsh, tidal creeks and two miles of white-sand beach at the northern tip of **Isle of Palms★**. Long before a bridge connected this barrier island to the mainland, the Seewee Indians called the island home. The first resort was built here in 1972 when the Sea Pines Company (which developed Hilton Head; *see p 148*) built the Isle of Palms Beach and Racquet Club on 1,600 acres of land at the north end of the island. New owners added a Tom Fazio-designed golf course (Wild Dunes Links) in 1980, and four years later the resort's name was changed to Wild Dunes Beach and Racquet Club.

Accommodations here today range from the 93-room Boardwalk Inn *(see Must Stay)* to a wide variety of rental properties.

Resort Activities

There's plenty to occupy your time at Wild Dunes. Between golf, tennis, parasailing, kayaking, biking or just walking on the beach, there's no reason to be bored—unless you want to be.

Golf – Wild Dunes claims two championship golf courses *(see Musts for Outdoor Fun)*.

Tennis – The tennis center here has 17 Har-Tru courts, five of which are lit for night play. Wild Dunes was rated among the top 10 tennis resorts in the US by *Tennis Magazine* in 2003.

Recreation – Adults can choose from working out at the fitness center, taking kayak tours, boating or parasailing. Day camps amuse the little ones with sand-castle building, scavenger hunts and field trips. For teens, the resort sponsors beach volleyball, pool parties, and even a surfing clinic.

Fun Fact

During the Revolutionary War, a cadre of 2,000 men under the command of Britain's Lord Cornwallis landed on Isle of Palms intending to cross Breach Inlet to Sullivan's Island and launch a surprise attack on Fort Moultrie. The place where they made landfall is now the 18th hole at the Wild Dunes Links golf course. (Oh, and, yes, the Patriot army was victorious in holding the British at bay on Isle of Palms).

Kiawah Island★★

21mi south of Charleston. Take the James Island Expressway and turn right on Folly Rd. Go left on Maybank Hwy. (Rte. 700) to Bohicket Rd. Turn left on Bohicket Rd., following signs to Kiawah Island. Turn left on Kiawah Island Pkwy. and proceed to the entrance gate. 843-768-2121 or 800-576-1570. www.kiawahresort.com.

Named for the Indians who hunted and fished here for hundreds of years before the first Europeans arrived, Kiawah Island embraces 10,000 breathtaking acres of maritime forest and pristine tidal marsh. In the 18C, the island was first owned by Revolutionary War hero General Arnoldus Vanderhorst, who raised Sea Island cotton here. After the Civil War, the land knew a succession of different owners until 1974, when it was developed as a resort and residential community.

Today Kiawah's ten miles of uninterrupted white beach provide plenty of space for relaxation. The newest addition to the beach is **The Sanctuary** *(see Must Stay and Must Be Pampered)*, a luxurious oceanfront hotel and spa, opened in August 2004 to round out the offerings of this world-class resort.

Kamp Kiawah

Need some private time? Don't feel guilty about dropping the kids off at Kamp Kiawah. Kids age 3 to 11 will stay entertained here with the likes of pirate adventures, crabbing, sand sculpting, crafts and contests. And it's all supervised fun. *Full day $60; morning $37; afternoon $32; evening programs $40 (includes dinner). Reservations required: 843-768-6001.*

Bohicket Marina Village

Just off Kiawah Island and right outside the gates to private Seabrook Island, Bohicket Marina's location facing west on Haulover Creek makes it a great place to watch the sunset. While you're there, you can also browse the shops, have a bite in Rosebank Farms Café *(see Must Eat)*, take a cruise, go parasailing, or rent a boat.

Resort Activities

If you're tired of sunbathing, try championship golf and tennis, bike the trails around the island or take the kids to the playground or pool at 21-acre Night Heron Park. In case you consider eating to be a sport, there are 10 restaurants to choose from on the resort grounds.

Golf – Kiawah's five scenic golf courses, which include the world-renowned Ocean Course, were designed by some of the biggest names in golf *(see Musts for Outdoor Fun)*.

Tennis – Two tennis centers on the property include 23 clay courts and 5 hard courts. There's even a practice court with a machine that will retrieve your balls for you. Tennis pro Roy Barth, a member of the Southern Tennis Hall of Fame, has been on staff here since 1976.

Recreation – In addition to the island's 30 miles of bike paths (you can rent bikes at Night Heron Park), Kiawah's Nature Excursion Program hosts naturalist-led canoe trips, sea-kayaking excursions and bird walks.

Shops at Kiawah – Kids love to come to West Beach Village to get ice cream and browse in the gift shops; adults can shop for beachwear (check out the end-of-season sales) and savor the catch of the day at Shrimper's Restaurant. And if you didn't pick up a Kiawah T-shirt at any of the tennis or golf pro shops on the island, you can get one here.

Wildlife, Wildlife, Everywhere

You'll share Kiawah's semi-tropical paradise with a host of wild critters:

Flocks of egrets, great blue herons, osprey and myriad other **waterbirds** feed in the marshes in the early morning and at dusk. Plan a walk or a bike ride and don't forget your binoculars.

You're likely to see **deer** on the island at any time of day—but especially after dusk—so be sure to heed posted speed limits. You'll also spy some good-size **alligators** sunning themselves on the banks of Kiawah's many ponds and waterways. They normally keep to themselves, as long as you don't bother them. Never, ever, feed an alligator! They become dangerous once they start associating humans with food; it seems that the reptiles' small brains don't distinguish between the food in your hand and your hand itself. And sluggish-looking gators can sprint at speeds nearing 15mph for distances of 50 yards—that's faster than you can run!

The Lowcountry Coast

Beaufort★

70mi south of Charleston via US-17 to US-21 South. Visitor information: 843-986-5400 or www.beaufortsc.org.

If Beaufort looks familiar to you, it's probably because the town has starred as the backdrop in so many movies—*The Big Chill, Forrest Gump, The Prince of Tides* and *The Legend of Bagger Vance*, to name a few. Its palmetto-lined streets, gracious architecture, moss-draped live oaks and flat tidal marshes make it the quintessential Southern setting.

The walkable 304-acre historic district takes in the entire original town of Beaufort (pronounced BYEW-furt), chartered as part of Britain's Carolina colony in 1711. Spend a leisurely day here to get an intimate look at the wealth generated by South Carolina's 18C and 19C planter class. To get a quick rundown of the city's history, pop into the **Beaufort Arsenal Museum** *(713 Craven St.; 843-525-7466; www.historic-beaufort.org; open Mon–Tue & Thu–Sat 10am–5pm; closed Wed & major holidays; $3).*

> ### Touring Tip
>
> Leave your car at **Waterfront Park** *(Bay & Newcastle Sts.)*, where restaurants, a covered market and a marina line the Beaufort River. Bordering the park, Bay Street teems with bookstores, shops and restaurants as well as some of the city's loveliest historic homes, most of which are privately owned. Walking-tour brochures are available at the **Beaufort Chamber of Commerce Visitors Center** *(1106 Carteret St.; open year-round daily 9am–5:30pm; closed major holidays).*

John Verdier House Museum – *801 Bay St. 843-379-6335. www.historic-beaufort.org. Visit by 30-minute guided tour only year-round Mon–Sat 10am–4pm. Closed Sun & major holidays. $5.* Washington may not have slept in this late-18C Federal-style house, but the Marquis de Lafayette did, in 1825. Merchant John Verdier's home illustrates the "Beaufort style"—with its raised first floor, double piazza, T-shaped floor plan, and shallow, hipped roof—designed to take full advantage of prevailing river breezes.

Spanish Moss

You see it everywhere in the Lowcountry, hanging like fringe over the branches of live oak and cypress trees. A symbol of the South, Spanish moss is quite the misnomer: it's neither Spanish, nor moss. It is, in fact, an epiphyte, or air plant, which wraps its long silvery-green stems around a host tree and drapes from the tree's branches. The plant's narrow leaves are covered with scales that trap moisture and nutrients from the air. In the 18C, Spanish moss was used in many Southern households to stuff mattresses. The insects that were often trapped in this natural filler became known as bed bugs, as in "don't let the bed bugs bite."

Penn School National Historic Landmark District

6.3mi southeast of Beaufort on St. Helena Island. From Beaufort, take US-21 South and turn right at Martin Luther King Jr. Dr. 843-838-2432. www.penncenter.com.

A short distance from Beaufort, Penn School Historic District makes an easy and worthwhile excursion. The 17 buildings here focus on the school established in 1862 by Philadelphia Quakers Laura Towne and Ellen Murray to educate Sea Island slaves freed at the beginning of the Civil War, before emancipation.

> **Touring Tip**
>
> Plan a visit on the second weekend in November to celebrate **Penn Center Heritage Days**, a three-day festival devoted to the unique cultural heritage of the Gullah people.

The Red Piano Too Art Gallery

870 Sea Island Pkwy./US-21. 843-838-2241. www.redpianotoo.com. A trip to St. Helena Island just isn't complete without a visit to The Red Piano Too. The best local enclave for Gullah art, the gallery is jam-packed with paintings, sculpture and decorative folk art by more than 100 Southern self-taught artists. Even if you don't buy anything, you'll get a good feel for the Gullah culture here.

York W. Bailey Museum – *110 Martin Luther King, Jr. Dr., St. Helena Island. 843-838-2474. Open year-round Mon–Sat 11am–4pm. Closed Sun & major holidays. $4.* In keeping with the historic district's mission to "promote and preserve Sea Island history and culture," the museum's permanent exhibit, Education for Freedom, highlights photographs, African artifacts and oral history recordings that interpret the impact that the Penn Center had on this coastal community.

The Language That Time Forgot

Yuh duh talk en Gullah? (Do you speak Gullah?) On the sea islands of South Carolina and Georgia, they do. These islands are home to a small community of African Americans who speak **Gullah**, remnants of a language and a way of life passed on from the early slaves who worked the plantations on the mainland. Kidnapped from their homelands and unable to communicate with whites or with each other, the slaves created a unique language based on their different West African tongues. Also referred to as Geechee, this creole dialect incorporates the vocabulary and grammar from the West African languages of Vai, Mende, Twi and Ewe, peppered with words from English, Spanish and Dutch, among others. The solitude experienced by slaves, who were relatively isolated on the coastal islands, facilitated the preservation of many African customs from storytelling and medicine to folk arts. Gullah strongholds remain on St. Helena, Daufuskie Island *(off the southern tip of Hilton Head)* and Sapelo Island *(Georgia State Parks department offers tours of Sapelo Island; for information, call 912-485-2299 or check online at gastateparks.org/info/sapelo).*

Hunting Island State Park ★

16mi east of Beaufort via US-21 South. 843-838-2011. www.discoversouthcarolina.com/stateparks. Open year-round daily dawn–dusk. $3 (free for children ages 15 and under).

True to its name, this beautiful barrier island was once used as a hunting ground. Now it's a 5,000-acre recreation spot for thousands of visitors each year. Palmetto trees and semi-tropical maritime forest edge the 4 miles of pristine beach. Anglers can cast their lines off the fishing pier (southern part of island), which extends 1,120 feet into Fripp Inlet. Nature lovers will want to walk the park's trails and look for seahorses in the man-made lagoon or try to catch a glimpse of pelicans, egrets, oystercatchers, wood storks and myriad other bird species that frequent this area. If you can't tear yourself away, reserve one of the park's 200 campground sites or its 14 cabins.

Lighthouse – *Closed to public for restoration; call to check status before you visit.* Confederate forces destroyed the 1859 lighthouse that once stood here so the Union army couldn't use it as a navigation aid. Rebuilt in 1875, the light towers 132 feet above the inlet. When it reopens to the public, you can climb the 167 steps to the top for a panoramic view of the island and the Atlantic Ocean.

> **Touring Tip**
>
> If you want to picnic at the beach, stop off along the way at one of the many produce stands, seafood shops or Gullah restaurants that line US-21, and get something to go.

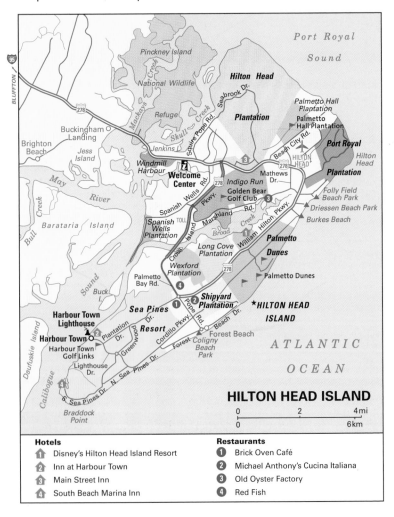

Hilton Head Island★

30mi south of Beaufort via I-95 South to US-278 East. Visitor information: 843-785-3673 or www.hiltonheadisland.org.

With its resorts, golf courses and tennis courts hidden amid 42 square miles of natural marshland, beach and maritime forest, Hilton Head ranks as one of South Carolina's most popular vacation destinations. The island's namesake is English explorer William Hilton, who sailed into Calibogue Sound in 1863. Development began almost a century later, when the two bridges connecting Hilton Head Island to the mainland opened in the mid-1950s. Today Hilton Head's 11 planned residential communities, many named for the antebellum plantations that once occupied their sites, take up more than half of the island.

HILTON HEAD ISLAND

0   2   4mi

0   6km

Hotels

1. Disney's Hilton Head Island Resort
2. Inn at Harbour Town
3. Main Street Inn
4. South Beach Marina Inn

Restaurants

1. Brick Oven Café
2. Michael Anthony's Cucina Italiana
3. Old Oyster Factory
4. Red Fish

Resorts

Here's a quick run-down of the resort communities that welcome vacationers:

Hilton Head Plantation – *7 Surrey Lane. 843-681-8800. www.hiltonhead plantation.com.* On the northern tip of the island, this 4,000-acre community boasts four 18-hole golf courses, a 180-slip marina, and a beach on Calibogue Sound.

Palmetto Dunes – *430 William Hilton Pkwy. 800-972-0257. www.palmettodunes.com.* Here, you can choose your accommodations: rent a house or villa, or stay in one of two resorts—the Marriott Beach Golf Resort or the Hilton Oceanfront. Palmetto Dunes' three courses are all open to the public.

Port Royal Plantation – *10A Grasslawn Ave. 843-681-9325. www.portroyal village.com.* One-and-a-half miles of Atlantic beach border Port Royal, which incorporates the site of the original Hilton Head bluff. The Port Royal Racquet Club and the Westin Resort Hilton Head are also located here.

Sea Pines Resort – *32 Greenwood Dr. 843-785-3333. www.seapines.com.* Located on the south end of the island, Sea Pines is the first (1957) and the largest (5,200 acres) of Hilton Head's residential communities. Amenities include Harbour Town village, 5 miles of beach and three public golf courses.

Shipyard Plantation – *Shipyard Dr. 843-785-3310. www.shipyardplantation.com.* The 834-acre plantation encompasses the Shipyard Golf Club, the Crowne Plaza Resort Hotel, and the Van der Meer Shipyard Tennis Resort.

Touring Tip

Most of the commercial amenities (restaurants, gas stations, hotels, shopping centers, and the entrance to several of the developments) on the island are located along William Hilton Parkway (US-278). It runs 11 miles from the northern end of the island down to Sea Pines Circle. On your way in, stop and pick up a map and information at the **Hilton Head/Bluffton Chamber of Commerce Welcome Center** *(100 William Hilton Pkwy., just past mile marker 1).* Note that addresses here can be difficult to find, given the island's strict ordinances that prohibit neon signs and limit the height of commercial buildings.

Harbour Town Lighthouse

149 Lighthouse Rd. 843-671-2810. www.harbourtownlighthouse .com. A Hilton Head landmark, the hexagonal, red-and-white-striped lighthouse marks the northern point of Harbour Town's yacht basin. The working light is not operated by the government; it was built in 1970 by the developers of Sea Pines. Towering 93 feet above Calibogue Sound, the light serves as a beacon for local sailors and fishermen. Climb the 110 steps up to the observation deck for a sweeping view of the island, and while you're there, pop into the gift shop.

Golf

Hilton Head has 25 golf courses, 17 of which are open to the public. All of Hilton Head's courses are either located within, or associated with, one of the planned communities. Resort greens fees are on the expensive side, but they vary depending on the course, the season, the day of the week, and the time of day you play. You'll often get the best deals in off-season, which in the resort area is from late-November through February. We've listed a sampling of courses below; for a complete list, check online: www.golfisland.com.

Golden Bear Golf Club – *72 Golden Bear Way, Indigo Run. 843-689-2200. www.goldenbear-indigorun.com.* Walking is allowed on this semi-private course, named for its designer, the Golden Bear, Jack Nicklaus.

Harbour Town Golf Links Course – *32 Greenwood Dr., Sea Pines. 888-807-6873. www.seapines.com.* The renowned Pete Dye-designed links hosts the PGA's MCI Heritage tournament every April.

Palmetto Dunes – *7 Trent Jones Lane. 843-785-1138. www.palmettodunes.com.* Choose among three courses at Palmetto Dunes: the wooded Arthur Hills course, the lagoon-laden Robert Trent Jones course, and the par-70 George Fazio course.

Palmetto Hall Plantation – *108 Fort Howell Dr. 843-785-1138. www.palmettodunes.com.* The popular Arthur Hills course here alternates public/private every day with its sister links, the Robert Cupp course.

Hilton Head Shopping

With some 200 shops on the island, you have no excuse not to pick up a few souvenirs for the folks back home. Sea Pines resort includes more than 20 gift and apparel shops at charming **Harbour Town**, on the north side of Harbour Town yacht basin *($5 entry fee if you're not staying at the resort; 843-363-5655; www.harbourtown.com).* You'll find discounts on designer duds including Dana Buchman, Jones New York, Polo Ralph Lauren and Geoffrey Beene at **Hilton Head Outlets** on US-278, located at the gateway to the island *(1414 Fording Island Rd.; 843-837-4339; www.tangeroutlet.com/centers).* If it's a mall you want, head for the enclosed **Mall at Shelter Cove** *(24 Shelter Cove Rd.; 843-686-3090; www.mallatsheltercove.com),* where you'll find chain stores from Victoria's Secret to Saks Fifth Avenue.

Tennis

Tennis is a popular pastime on Hilton Head, and there are plenty of places to play—more than 300 courts, in fact. Here are a few where the public can reserve a court:

Port Royal Racquet Club – *15 Wimbledon Ct., Port Royal Plantation. 843-686-8803. www.portroyalplantation.com.* You'll find all three surface types on Port Royal's courts: 16 clay courts, 4 hard-surface courts and 2 grass courts.

Sea Pines Racquet Club – *5 Lighthouse Lane, Sea Pines. 843-785-8388. www.seapines.com.* This highly rated club is home to the renowned Stan Smith Tennis Academy.

Van Der Meer Shipyard Tennis Resort – *116 Shipyard Dr., Shipyard Plantation. 843-686-8804. www.shipyardplantation.com.* Owned by tennis instructor Dennis Van Der Meer, Shipyard's tennis resort boasts 20 championship courts.

Daufuskie Island Resort

Access by the resort's cruise boat from the Embarkation Center on Hilton Head Island. Follow US-278 over the Hilton Head Bridge. Take a left at the first traffic light onto Squire Pope Rd. Go about 2mi to the Daufuskie Island Embarkation Center, on the left. Boats depart on even hours, beginning at 8am. No cars are permitted on the island; golf carts and bicycles are the only vehicles allowed. You can take a shuttle to your accommodations or rent a golf cart. 843-842-2000. www.daufuskieresort.com.

Here's a place to escape the crowds and high-rise condominiums on Hilton Head. Once known for its Sea Island cotton and the oysters that were harvested from its waters, 8-square-mile Daufuskie Island is now home to a resort that provides a quiet respite from the daily grind.

For accommodations, take your pick among Queen Anne-style rooms at the **Melrose Inn**, family-friendly beachside cottages, or 3-bedroom, 3-bath villas. Four restaurants cater to all tastes, from the eclectic menu at the casual Beach Club to the Mediterranean-inspired fare and extensive wine list at the Melrose Inn's Stoddard Bistro.

If it's action you want, there are two 18-hole golf courses with great views of the Atlantic, the Jack Nicklaus signature Melrose course, and the Bloody Point links, named after a notorious 18C battle fought here between the Native Americans and the British. Then there's horseback riding—a great way to see the beach—kayaking, parasailing, jet skiing, tennis, and the beach club with its two swimming pools and fitness center.

Prefer to relax? At the **Breathe Spa** your personal spa coordinator can help you choose among 45 separate treatments. Of course, the beach beckons nearby with the gentle hiss of the surf, or simply claim one of the beachside hammocks and let the breeze rock you to sleep.

It's only a couple of hours down the coast from Charleston to the romantic Southern city of Savannah, with its landscaped squares and eccentric ways. Another hour or so brings you to Georgia's fabled Golden Isles, a vacationer's paradise of golf courses, beaches and wildlife refuges.

Savannah★★

Tourist information: 877-728-2662 or www.savannahvisit.com. For practical information, see p 17.

With its stately mansions, landscaped squares, Spanish-moss-draped live oaks and friendly residents, Savannah, Georgia is a quintessentially Southern city. The city was born in 1733 when English army officer and philanthropist **James Oglethorpe** and a group of more than 100 settlers landed at Yamacraw Bluff above the Savannah River. One of 21 trustees to whom King George II had granted the tract of land between the Savannah and Altamaha rivers, Oglethorpe envisioned the colony of Georgia as a place where the British working poor and "societal misfits" could carve out a living cultivating agricultural products desired by the Crown.

In its early years, the region's economy, based on rice and tobacco and, later, cotton, fueled Savannah's growth as a port and a center for commodities trading. By 1817 Savannah's City Exchange was setting the market price for the world's cotton.

Of course, that all ended with the Civil War. When General Sherman finally reached Savannah in December 1864, city leaders surrendered without a fight. Sherman, acknowledging the city's beauty, presented Savannah to President Abraham Lincoln as a Christmas gift.

Southern charm now pervades this eccentric city, which perches on a bluff above the river, as a testimony to visionary 18C city planning and modern historic preservation.

St. Patrick's Day in Savannah

You might think it's Mardi Gras when you see the revelry with which Savannah's residents celebrate St. Patrick's Day. The squares aren't the only things that are green on March 17; they dye the water in the fountains and the beer in the bars green, too. Savannah's St. Patrick's Day celebration began in 1813 with the Irish Hibernian Society. Today the two-hour-long parade through the historic district and the River Street bacchanalia that follows attract hearty partyers from around the country. *For details, call 912-233-4804 or check online at savannahga.gov/cityweb/stpat/index.html.*

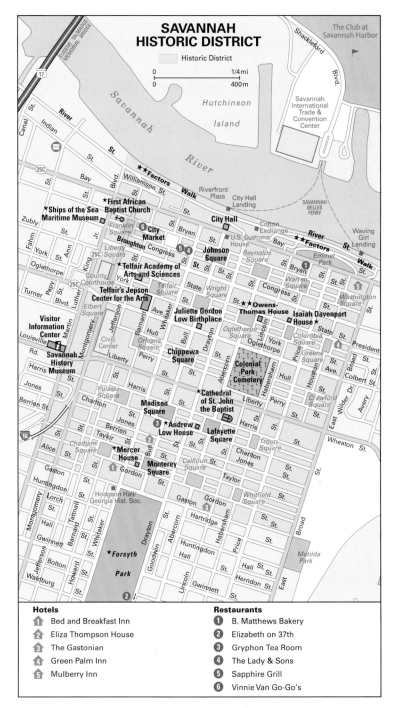

SAVANNAH HISTORIC DISTRICT

Historic District

0 ⎯⎯ 1/4mi
0 ⎯⎯ 400m

The Club at Savannah Harbor

Shackleford

Blvd.

EUGENE TALMADGE MEMORIAL BRIDGE

17

Savannah International Trade & Convention Center

Hutchinson Island

Savannah River

Canal St.
Indian St.
River St.
Bay St.
25C
Zubly St.
Fahm St.
York St.
Oglethorpe St.
Turner Papy
Louisville Rd.
Harris St.
Jones St.
Berrien St.
Alice St.
Gaston St.
Huntingdon St.
Lorch St.
Hall St.
Gwinnett St.
Waldburg St.
Bolton St.
Jefferson St.
Howard St.

Williamson St.
★★Factors Walk
Riverfront Plaza
City Hall Landing
SAVANNAH BELLES FERRY

★Ships of the Sea Maritime Museum
★First African Baptist Church
Franklin Square
City Market
Broughton St.
Congress St.
Liberty Square
★Telfair Academy of Arts and Sciences
Telfair's Jepson Center for the Arts
Elbert Square
Visitor Information Center
Civic Center
Orleans Square
Savannah History Museum
Pulaski Square
Madison Square
Chatham Square
★Mercer House
Monterey Square
Hodgson Hall/ Georgia Hist. Soc.
★Forsyth Park

City Hall
Cotton Exchange
U.S. Customs House
★★River Factors
Bryan St.
Johnson Square
Reynolds Square
State St.
Wright Square
Telfair Square
Hull St.
Chippewa Square
★Juliette Gordon Low Birthplace
★★Owens-Thomas House
Oglethorpe Square
York St.
Isaiah Davenport House
Columbia Square
Greene Square
Colonial Park Cemetery
★Cathedral of St. John the Baptist
Lafayette Square
★Andrew Low House
Troup Square
Crawford Square
Washington Square
Emmet Park
Waving Girl Landing
★★River Factors
Walk

Bull St.
Drayton St.
Abercorn St.
Lincoln St.
Habersham St.
Price St.
Houston St.
Broad St.
East Broad St.
East Wilder Dr.
Avery St.
Wheaton St.
Matilda Park

Whitfield Square
Gordon St.
Gaston St.
Hartridge St.
Huntingdon St.
Hall St.
Herndon St.
Gwinnett St.

Historic District★★

James Oglethorpe's revered original city plan incorporated a perfect grid of broad thoroughfares punctuated by 24 grassy squares (three have been lost to urban sprawl). Bull Street cuts down the center of the grid, from twenty-acre **Forsyth Park★**, with its graceful fountain, to gold-domed City Hall.

Edged with handsome 19C examples of Greek Revival, Federal, Regency and Georgian architecture, Oglethorpe's streets and squares are now preserved in the 2.5-mile downtown historic district *(bounded by Gaston St., E Broad St., Martin Luther King Jr. Blvd. and the river)*.

Touring Tip: Exploring the Historic District

Check in first at the **Savannah Visitor Information Center** *(301 Martin Luther King Jr. Blvd.; 912-944-0455; open year-round Mon–Fri 8:30am–5pm, weekends 9am–5pm)*, where you can catch one of the popular narrated **trolley tours** of the historic downtown. If you want a quick overview of the city's past, stop in the adjoining **Savannah History Museum** *(912-651-6825; www.chsgeorgia.org; same hours as visitor center; $4)*.

Factors Walk★★

West Factors Walk lines Bay St. between Whitaker & Montgomery Sts.; East Factors Walk is on Bay St. between Lincoln & Houston Sts.

Riverfront warehouses along Bay Street make up Factors Walk, hub of cotton commerce in the 19C. Here cotton traders, called factors, would buy and sell from the bridgeways that connect the offices on the upper portion of the bluff—the two-story buildings that face Bay Street—with the warehouses on River Street below. Walk down the steep steps to **River Street**, where restored 19C warehouses now contain a dizzying array of shops and restaurants.

City Hall

Separating East and West Factors Walk, 1905 City Hall *(1 Bay St. at Bull St.)* reigns as a vibrant local landmark with its 70-foot-high dome, covered in 23-karat gold leaf. City Hall stands on the site of the Old City Exchange, which set the market price for the world's cotton in the days before the Civil War. A **stone bench** in front of the building commemorates Oglethorpe's landing on this bluff in 1733.

Owens-Thomas House★★

124 Abercorn St. 912-233-9743. www.telfair.org. Visit by 45-minute guided tour only, year-round Mon noon–5pm, Tue–Sat 10am–5pm, Sun 1pm–5pm. Closed major holidays. $8.

The belle of Oglethorpe Square, Owens-Thomas House is considered one of architect William Jay's finest works—and the only unaltered example of his surviving designs. Now administered by the Telfair Academy of Arts and Sciences, this house was completed in 1819 for cotton merchant Richard Richardson when the architect was only 25. The stately structure typifies the English Regency style; its tabby and coadestone exterior as well as the elegant interior—adorned with the likes of Duncan Phyfe furniture and a brass-inlaid staircase—have been carefully restored. Out back, the carriage house includes one of the earliest intact urban slave quarters in the South.

Andrew Low House★

329 Abercorn St. 912-233-6854. www.andrewlowhouse.com. Visit by 30-minute guided tour only, year-round Mon–Wed, Fri & Sat 10am–4:30pm; Sun noon–4:30pm. Closed Thu & major holidays. $7.

In 1848 wealthy cotton merchant Andrew Low commissioned John Norris to create this Classical-style house with its elaborate cast-iron balconies. Low's son, William, married Savannah-born **Juliette Gordon Low** (1860–1927), who founded the Girl Scouts here on March 12, 1912. Located in back of the residence, the Low's carriage house served as the first headquarters of the Girl Scouts USA—the world's largest voluntary organization for girls. Juliette Gordon Low died at Low House in 1927. Today Low family pieces and period antiques fill the rooms.

It's Hip To Be A Square

. . . At least it is in Savannah, which owes its famed layout of gracious squares to founder James Oglethorpe. Here are some highlights among the city's 21 existing landscaped plazas:

Chippewa Square – *Bull St. between Hull & Perry Sts.* Hollywood immortalized this square as the one in which Forrest Gump sat waiting for the bus. A statue of Savannah founder James Oglethorpe by Daniel Chester French marks the center of the plaza.

Johnson Square – *Bull St. between Bryan & Congress Sts.* Oldest of the city's squares, Johnson Square was laid out in 1733.

Lafayette Square – *Abercorn St. between E. Harris & E. Charleton Sts.* A three-tiered fountain sits in the middle of this square, named for—you guessed it—the Marquis de Lafayette.

Madison Square – *Bull St. between W. Harris & W. Charleton Sts.* President James Madison is the namesake of this plaza. The statue here commemorates Revolutionary War hero Sgt. William Jasper.

Monterey Square – *Bull St. between Taylor & Gordon Sts.* Monterey Square boasts a monument (1854) honoring General Casimir Pulaski, who was mortally wounded near this spot during the 1779 Siege of Savannah.

Cathedral of St. John the Baptist★

222 E. Harris St. 912-233-4709. www.savannahcathedral.org.
Open year-round Mon–Fri 9am–5pm. Closed weekends.

You'll recognize the seat of Savannah's Catholic diocese
by the twin spires that tower over the historic district.
Dedicated in 1876, this French Gothic cathedral dates back
to a parish established in Savannah in the late 1700s. Step
inside to see the results of the four-year restoration
project (completed in 2000), which restored the cathedral's Austrian
stained-glass windows and Italian marble altar to their former glory.

Isaiah Davenport House★

324 E. State St. 912-236-8097. www.davenportsavga.com. Visit by 30-minute guided tour
only, year-round Mon–Sat 10am–4pm, Sun 1pm–4pm (last tour starts at 4pm). $7.

Designed and constructed by Rhode Island master
builder Isaiah Davenport, this fine two-story brick Federal structure was completed in 1820. When threatened
by demolition in the 1950s, the house overlooking
Columbia Square became a rallying point for citizens
interested in preserving Savannah's stately homes. The
community effort resulted in both saving the home and
establishing the Historic Savannah Foundation, a grassroots organization that
has played a key role in the rejuvenation of the historic district.

Ships of the Sea Maritime Museum★

41 Martin Luther King Jr. Blvd. 912-232-1511. www.shipsofthesea.org. Open year-round
Tue–Sun 10am–5pm. Closed Mon & major holidays. $7.

A block west of City Market, a charming garden invites visitors into Scar-
brough House, an 1819 Regency villa designed by famed English architect
William Jay. Today the villa houses a maritime museum, which presents nau-
tical history and seafaring culture through a fine selection of artifacts, paintings and model ships encompassing the period from the earliest days of sail to
World War II.

Broughton Street Shopping

Let's face it, shopping along the riverfront is fine if you want T-
shirts and Savannah-emblazoned souvenirs, but you'll find more
interesting shops along Broughton Street, from Bull Street to
Martin Luther King, Jr. Boulevard. Here are a few examples:
Go Fish – *106 W. Broughton St. 912-231-0609. www.gofishretail.
com.* Casual women's clothing takes on beachy prints.
Clipper Trading Company – *201 W. Broughton St. 912-238-3660.
www.clippertrading.com.* A world of imports from around the
globe fill the former headquarters of Silver's 5 & 10¢ Store.
Wonderful Things – *115 W. Broughton St. 912-447-0004. www.wonderfulthingsinc.com.*
Fine bed linens and accessories here make for sweet dreams.
The Beadstro – *226 W. Broughton St. 912-232-2334. www.info.beadstro.com.* String
your own jewelry from bins and bins of beads.

Telfair Academy of Arts and Sciences★

121 Barnard St. 912-232-1177. www.telfair.org. Open year-round Mon noon–5pm, Tue–Sat 10am–5pm, Sun 1pm–5pm. Closed major holidays. $8.

Another creation of William Jay, the Regency-style mansion was built in 1818 as the home of Alexander Telfair. The expanded structure now houses 19C and 20C American and European paintings and portraiture, including a note-worthy group of works by members of the Ash Can school—Robert Henri, George Luks and George Bellows. Located on the entrance level you'll find two period rooms. The Octagon Room, with its 19C Grecian couches and faux oak paneling, was Telfair's reception room; the Dining Room showcases a Duncan Phyfe mahogany sideboard and early 19C English silver.

Next door, the new 64,000-square-foot **Telfair's Jepson Center for the Arts** will house the academy's collection of 20C and 21C art when it opens in fall 2005.

City Market

Jefferson St. at W. St. Julian St. 912-232-4903. www.savannahcitymarket.com.

There's always something doing at City Market. Listen to live music, catch a carriage tour, sample the shops or relax at the outdoor cafes at this lively marketplace.

Across Montgomery Street from the market, **First African Baptist Church★** *(23 Montgomery St.; 912-233-6597)* is considered the oldest black Baptist church in North America; it was established in 1773 by freed slave George Leile. The current structure was built in 1859 by members of the congregation.

Colonial Park Cemetery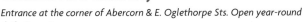

Entrance at the corner of Abercorn & E. Oglethorpe Sts. Open year-round daily 8am–5pm.

Inside the gates of Colonial Park you'll find some of Savannah's most distinguished citizens—the deceased ones, that is. Savannah's second cemetery opened in 1750; the last body was buried here in 1853. Tucked amid the live oaks you'll find the graves of James Habersham, acting Royal Governor of the Province of Georgia from 1771–73; naval hero Capt. Denis Cottineau, who fought with John Paul Jones in 1779; and renowned 18C miniaturist Edward Greene Malbone. The cemetery has been a park since 1896.

Juliette Gordon Low Birthplace

10 E. Oglethorpe St. 912-233-4501. www.girlscouts.org/birthplace. Vist by 30-minute guided tour only, year-round Thu–Sat 10am–4pm, Sun 12:30pm–4:30pm. $7.

Girl Scouts from around the world make pilgrimages here to visit the childhood home of their founder, who was born in this house in 1860. Known as Daisy, Low was the second of six children born to cotton factor William Gordon II and his wife, Eleanor. The 1821 English Regency-style house has been painstakingly restored to reflect the year 1886, when Juliette Gordon married William Mackay Low.

Fort Pulaski National Monument★

14mi east of downtown Savannah via US-80, on Tybee Island. 912-786-5787. www.nps.gov/fopu. Open year-round daily 9am–5pm (until 7pm in summer). $3 (admission covers 7 days).

Named for Revolutionary War hero Casimir Pulaski, who lost his life defending the city of Savannah against the British, Fort Pulaski was built between 1833 and 1847. The battery saw most of its action during the Civil War, when Confederate troops sieged the fort even before Georgia seceded from the Union. In April 1862, Union forces recaptured the fort, using their experimental rifled cannon. They quickly sealed off the port of Savannah and held the fort for the rest of the war.

Fort Pulaski was declared a national monument in 1924. Today you can tour its restored ramparts, complete with cannon, moat and drawbridge. The 5,600-acre site includes picnic grounds and nature trails, with views of the Altantic Ocean in the distance.

Midnight in the Garden of Good and Evil

429 Bull St. 912-236-6352. www.mercerhouse.com. Visit by 30-minute guided tour only, year-round Mon–Sat 10:30am–4pm, Sun 12:30pm–4pm. $12.50. Tickets are available at the Mercer House Carriage Shop, 430 Whitaker St. A stately Italianate mansion overlooking Savannah's Monterey Square, the c.1860s **Mercer House★**—designed by New York architect John Norris— became famous as a crime scene. It was in this house in 1981 that resident antiques dealer Jim Williams was accused of fatally shooting 21-year-old Danny Hansford.

Jim Williams' murder trial set staid Savannah on its ear, and was later immortalized in John Berendt's best-selling 1994 book *Midnight in the Garden of Good and Evil.* Both the book and the movie that followed in 1997 painted a vivid picture of Savannah's eccentric populace. The most recognized icon from both the book and the movie is perhaps the sculpture *Bird Girl* (1938), which appears on the book's cover. The work of Sylvia Shaw Judson, the statue stands in the Telfair Academy of Arts and Sciences.

Georgia's Golden Isles★

Tourist information: 912-265-0620 or 800-933-2627; www.bgivb.com.
To reach the Golden Isles from Savannah, travel south on I-95 from Savannah to US-17 South. For practical information, see p 17.

Strung like shining beads along Georgia's Atlantic Coast, the Golden Isles—Sea Island, St. Simons Island, private Little St. Simons Island *(see p 159)*, and Jekyll Island—lie amid a setting of gold-green marshes, diamond-white sands and lapis-blue waters. These popular destinations, located 70 miles south of Savannah and boasting an average annual temperature of 68°F, attract thousands of visitors each year to play on the area's golf courses and tennis courts, visit its historic resorts, and relax on its wide sandy beaches.

Jekyll Island★★

From I-95, take Exit 29 and follow US-17 to the Jekyll Causeway. Jekyll Island Welcome Center is located on the causeway. 912-653-5955. www.jekyllisland.com. Open year-round daily 9am–5pm. There's a $3/vehicle fee to drive onto the island.

Dubbed "Georgia's Jewell," Jekyll Island grew up as a playground for America's millionaires—do the names Gould, Goodyear, Pulitzer and Rockefeller ring a bell? These men, and other East Coast captains of industry, formed a consortium in 1886 and purchased the island for $125,000. Here in 1887, consortium members—who called themselves the Jekyll Island Club—hired architect Charles Alexander to build a 60-room clubhouse (now the Jekyll Island Club Hotel). The wealthy financiers soon supplemented their clubhouse with "cottages," as they called their anything-but-modest winter retreats, which ranged up to 8,000 square feet in size.

World War II put an end to playtime in 1942, when the club closed. In 1947 the State of Georgia purchased the island, which today preserves Jekyll's historic structures within the 200-acre Jekyll Island Club National Historic Landmark District. The ocean side of the island is lined with hotels and beaches.

Brunswick Stew

First created in Brunswick, Georgia—the commercial hub of the Golden Isles and an important port in its own right—delectable Brunswick stew combines chicken, beef and pork, slow-simmered with local vegetables (tomatoes, butter beans, corn, potatoes and okra), herbs and spices. It's often served with fresh local shrimp, crab and oysters, and appears on many menus throughout the area. Be sure to sample some while you're in the area.

Jekyll Island National Historic Landmark District★★

Tours depart from the Museum Visitor Center in the old club stables (Stable Rd.). 912-635-4036. Tram tours: 45-minute overview (daily 10am & 4pm; $10) or 90-minute in-depth tour (daily 11am & 2pm; $17.50), which allows access to two cottages.

Restored as a resort hotel, the Queen Anne-style **Jekyll Island Club**, with its signature turret, now forms the centerpiece of the historic district *(371 Riverview Dr.; see Must Stay)*, along with the members' former cottages and outbuildings. Even the shops occupy historic structures: a bookstore fills a lovely white shingle cottage; the former powerhouse is being restored as a sea turtle center. Wander around at your leisure, or take in more of the area's history on one of the guided tram tours.

Cottages – Facing the Intracoastal Waterway amid moss-draped live oaks, 15 cottages were built by club members beginning in 1887. At that time, decades before a bridge linked Jekyll Island to the mainland, members arrived for the "club season" (January through March) via steamship or private yacht.

- **Goodyear Cottage**, built for lumber baron Frank Goodyear in 1906, is the only home open to the public on a regular basis *(Mon–Fri noon–4pm; weekends 10am–4pm)*.

- With 20 rooms and 13 baths, Italian Renaissance **Crane Cottage** (1917) was the grandest on the island; Crane and Cherokee (1904) cottages have both been restored as the latest additions to the hotel.

Faith Chapel – Constructed in 1904, little wooden Faith Chapel once held services for the members of the Jekyll Island Club. Stop in to see the chapel's striking stained-glass windows, designed by Louis Comfort Tiffany and D. Maitland Armstrong.

St. Simons Island★

77mi south of Savannah. From I-95, take Exit 9 and follow US-17 South to St. Simons Causeway.

Largest of the Golden Isles, St. Simons is known for its beautiful beaches as well as its colorful history. Beginning in 1736, when James Oglethorpe built Fort Frederica here, the English and Spanish struggled for control of the island. Oglethorpe attempted unsuccessfully to capture the Spanish fort in St. Augustine, Florida in 1740; the Spanish counterattack came two years later. During the **Battle of Bloody Marsh** in 1742, Oglethorpe and his forces soundly defeated the Spaniards, who retreated back to Florida (a small monument off Demere Road marks the battle site).

In the years before the Civil War, St. Simons was blanketed with cotton plantations, famous for their high-quality Sea Island cotton. Now resort hotels and golf clubs cover much of the former plantation land.

Village – The tiny village at the island's southern tip centers on Mallory Street *(off Kings Way/Ocean Blvd.)*. This is where you'll find shops and restaurants, as well as the public pier *(end of Mallory St.)*.

Fort Frederica National Monument★ – *At the end of Frederica Rd. 912-638-3639. www.nps.gov/fofr. Grounds open year-round daily 8am–5pm. Closed Dec 25. $5/vehicle, $3/ person on foot or bike.* James Oglethorpe and his soldiers built Fort Frederica in 1736 as Georgia's first military outpost. Today the ruins of the square fort and its earthen ramparts stand on a bend in the Frederica River.

St. Simons Lighthouse – *101 Twelfth St. 912-638-4666. www.saintsimonslighthouse.org. Open year-round Mon–Sat 10am–5pm, Sun 1:30pm–5pm. Closed Jan 1, Thanksgiving Day & Dec 24–25. $5.* Icon of the island, this 104-foot-tall working lighthouse stands near the pier, where it has guided sailors since 1872. Climb the 129 steps to the top of the lighthouse for a great **view** of the Golden Isles. The adjacent **Museum of Coastal History** exhibits artifacts from the area's maritime past.

> ### St. Simons Trolley
>
> *Departs from Neptune Park (at the end of Mallory St., next to the pier) mid-Mar–Sept daily 11am–1pm. Rest of the year daily 11am. 921-638-8954. www.stsimonstours.com. $18 adults; $10 children (ages 4-12).* This 90-minute narrated tram tour takes you all around St. Simons; along the way you'll learn the island's historical highlights.

Sea Island

Accessible via Sea Island Dr. from St. Simons Island.

Ohio automobile magnate Howard Coffin had a vision as he looked out across the undeveloped marshland of Sea Island in 1923. In his mind's eye, he imagined a resort and beachfront homes on the land that once held cotton plantations. Coffin's dream is a reality today; Sea Island, with its residential cottage community, has become synonymous with **The Cloister**, a world-class resort *(entrance off Sea Island Dr.; see Must Stay)* that occupies part of the island.

> ### Little St. Simons
>
> *Accessible only by boat from the Hampton River Club Marina on the north end of St. Simons Island, daily 10am & 4:30pm. 921-638-7472 or 888-733-5774. www.littlestsimonsisland.com.* Ten thousand acres of natural beauty and solitude are what you'll find at private Little St. Simons Island. No crowds disturb this tranquil spot; only 30 people at a time are permitted on the island. Purchased for its cedar trees in the early 1900s by pencil manufacturer Philip Berolzheimer, Little St. Simons now offers accommodations in a 1930s bungalow or in the elegantly appointed three-bedroom Helen House. Spend your days here canoeing the winding tidal creeks, biking the 15 miles of trails, or strolling the 7 miles of deserted beach.

Cumberland Island National Seashore★★

10mi southeast of Brunswick, via I-95 South. Take Exit 2 off I-95 and turn left on Rte. 40; follow Rte. 40 east 9mi to St. Marys, GA. Accessible by ferry only from downtown St. Marys (reservations required; see sidebar below). 912-882-4335 www.nps.gov/cuis.

Haven for wild horses, sea turtles, alligators, armadillos and a host of shorebirds, Cumberland Island National Seashore sprawls over 17.5 miles of saltwater marshes, maritime forests and lonely beaches. The largest and least developed of Georgia's barrier islands lies across Cumberland Sound from St. Marys, Georgia.

Several cotton plantations operated on the island before Thomas Carnegie (brother of Pittsburgh industrialist Andrew Carnegie) and his wife, Lucy, purchased 4,000 acres here in 1881. The secluded estate they constructed was used for hunting and entertaining guests. Carnegie descendants owned the land until 1972, when they donated most of their holdings to the National Park Service.

On the Island

Plum Orchard – *Visit by guided tour only. 912-882-4335.* Georgian Revival-style Plum Orchard was built in 1898 for Thomas Carnegie's son, George, and his wife. You can imagine the lavish lifestyle that the Carnegies enjoyed as you tour its partly furnished rooms.

Dungeness – The eerie ruins of the mansion Thomas and Lucy Carnegie built in 1884 now rise amid the island foliage.

Greyfield Inn – Another former Carnegie mansion, the rambling home built in 1900 for Margaret Ricketson, daughter of Thomas and Lucy Carnegie, now operates as an upscale inn *(see Must Stay)*.

The Scoop on Cumberland Island

Getting to Cumberland Island – Begin your visit on the mainland at Mainland Visitor Information Center *(107 St. Marys St.; 912-882-4336; open year-round daily 8:15am–4:30pm; closed Dec 25)*. Ferries leave from 107 W. St. Marys Street *(schedule varies seasonally; 912-882-4335; www.stmaryswelcome.com; $12 adults, $7 children)*. Day-use fee to visit Cumberland Island is $4/person. No supplies are available on the island.

Camping – You can camp year-round on Cumberland Island. Reservations are required for all camping on the island. Camping at both sites is limited to seven days. Fees do not include day use/ferry fees.

The four **backcountry** sites *($2/person/night)* have no facilities, and water should be treated. No campfires are permitted in the backcountry.

The developed campground at Sea Camp Beach *($4/person/night)* offers rest rooms, cold showers and drinking water. Each site is equipped with a grill, fire ring, food cage and picnic table.

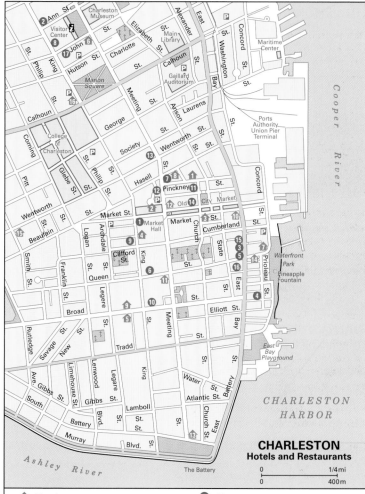

Hotels

1. Andrew Pinckney Inn
2. Charleston Place Hotel
3. French Quarter Inn
4. Fulton Lane Inn
5. Governor's House Inn
6. Hampton Inn Historic District
7. Harbour View Inn
8. Indigo Inn
9. John Rutledge House Inn
10. Market Pavilion Hotel
11. Mills House Hotel
12. Planters Inn
13. Two Meeting Street Inn
14. Vendue Inn
15. Wentworth Mansion
16. The Westin Francis Marion

Restaurants

1. Baker's Café
2. Basil's
3. Blossom
4. Carolina's
   Charleston Grill
5. Cypress
6. 82 Queen
7. FIG
8. Fish
9. Fulton Five
10. Gaulart & Maliclet
11. Hank's Seafood Restaurant
12. Hyman's Seafood Company
13. Jestine's Kitchen
14. Kaminsky's
15. Magnolias
16. McCrady's
    Peninsula Grill
17. 39 Rue de Jean

The venues listed below were selected for their ambience, location and/or value for money. Rates indicate the average cost of an appetizer, an entrée and a dessert for one person (not including tax, gratuity or beverages). Most restaurants are open daily (except where noted) and accept major credit cards. Call for information regarding reservations, dress code and opening hours.

$$$$	Over $50	$$	$15–$30
$$$	$30–$50	$	Under $15

Dining in the Charleston Area

Properties in this section are located in Charleston unless otherwise noted.

Luxury

Charleston Grill $$$$ New Southern

In the Charleston Place Hotel. 205 Meeting St. (main entrance off Hassell St.). Dinner only. 843-724-8410. www.charlestonplacehotel.com.

Celebrated chef Bob Waggoner's French training shines through in his superb Southern cuisine, which consistently wins raves from diners and food critics alike. His cassoulet is a Lowcountry blend of black-eyed peas, duck confit, boneless lamb ribs, homemade duck sausage and braised pork belly, while his interpretation of Frogmore stew yields a bowl filled with fresh shrimp, homemade andouille sausage, crabmeat and corn simmering in a shellfish broth. With its warm mahogany paneling, marble floors and oversize floral arrangements, the lovely dining room sets the stage for a meal to remember. The wine list offers more than 900 selections from around the world, with a focus on American, French and Italian varietals.

McCrady's $$$$ New American

2 Unity Alley, off E. Bay St. 843-577-0025. www.mccradysrestaurant.com.

Built in 1778, Charleston's first tavern retains its Old English style with timbered ceilings, wrought-iron light fixtures, arched door openings and its original brick walls. Executive chef Michael Kramer melds complex layers of flavors in wonderful dishes like local grouper with cauliflower, baby zucchini, lobster salad and Yuzu lemon butter; and Alaskan halibut with sunburst squash, baby carrots, pearl onions and truffle-corn emulsion. Although the dessert menu is bound to make your mouth water, the cheese-tasting course is tempting, too.

Woodlands Resort & Inn

$$$$ New American

125 Parsons Rd., Summerville. Dinner only. Closed Sun. 843-308-2115.
www.woodlandsinn.com. Jackets required.

Set in a residential neighborhood about a 20-minute drive
northwest of Charleston via I-26, the Woodlands makes a
great weekend getaway. Book yourself into one of the 19
luxurious rooms (**$$$-$$$$**) so you don't have to drive home
after dinner. Then get ready for a feast; "poetry on a plate" is
how the Charleston *Post and Courier* described the food

here. You'll have several prix-fixe menu options, from a four-course dinner (*$69*) to a
ten-course repast (*$99*) prepared at the whim of chef Scott Crawford. For that
really special occasion, you can reserve the special chef's table in the kitchen for
$120 per person.

Moderate

Atlanticville

$$$ Southern

2063 Middle St., Sullivan's Island. Dinner & Sun brunch. 843-883-9452.
www.atlanticville.net.

Located along Sullivan's little restaurant strip, Atlanticville feels like your aunt's old
beach house, with its paneled walls, Victorian décor and white tablecloths. The
food, on the other hand, puts a Lowcountry spin on contemporary cuisine—whole
fried flounder with John's Island squash casserole and collards; sautéed shrimp and
scallops with yellow-tomato and avocado gazpacho; truffled mac and cheese. It's
also a nice place for a quiet Sunday brunch.

Blossom

$$$ Lowcountry

171 E. Bay St. 843-722-9200. www.magnolias-blossom-cypress.com.

Magnolias' casual little sister recently celebrated its tenth anniversary by rein-
venting itself. Instead of Italian food, this lively spot now features Lowcountry fare,
with a focus on seafood. Seared or grilled yellowfin tuna, Carolina crab ravioli,
cornmeal-crusted catfish, and barbecue snapper are just a few of the tempting
new selections. Fans of the former menu will be glad to know that Blossom still
offers those crispy wood-oven pizzas and several house-made pastas. In nice
weather, grab a seat outside on the patio.

The Boathouse at Breach Inlet $$$ Seafood

101 Palm Blvd., Isle of Palms. Dinner only. 843-886-8000. www.boathouserestaurants.com.

There's always a crowd at this pleasant waterfront seafood place. "Simply fresh seafood" is their mantra here, where fish such as ahi tuna, black grouper and Atlantic salmon are grilled with your choice of sauces. The signature dish, lobster and crab cake (three petit coldwater lobster tails served with one of the restaurant's yummy jumbo lump crab cakes) also comes in variations with filet mignon. Come in time to watch the sunset over Breach Inlet from your table or from the rooftop bar. There's a Boathouse in Charleston, too *(549 E. Bay St.)*, but it can't compare with the Isle of Palms setting.

Carolina's $$$ Lowcountry

10 Exchange St. Dinner only. 843-724-3800. www.carolinasrestaurant.com.

Regional seafood stars in this casual-chic dining room, which was given a facelift with pecky cypress beams, antique mirrors and custom lighting and tiles in early 2004. Executive chef Rose Durden, aka "Mama Rose," has been presiding over the kitchen in the 18C structure for 16 years. Appetizers like black-eyed pea cakes or macadamia-nut fried Carolina quail, and entrées such as local grouper crusted with almonds and black sesame seeds, and Charleston seafood pot (shrimp, scallops, calamari, fish, mussels and clams in a tomato-saffron broth) all reflect the Lowcountry's culinary heritage—and are guaranteed to please your palate.

Cypress $$$ American

167 E. Bay St. Dinner only. 843-727-0111. www.magnolias-blossom-cypress.com.

Occupying an 1834 building with exposed brick walls and high ceilings, this sleek eatery packs in locals and visitors alike for regional cuisine with an Asian twist. Complement seared mahi-mahi, hickory-grilled filet of beef or smoked-salmon Wellington with your choice of wine from the 4,500 bottles lining the three-story wine wall. Tableside preparations for two—Chateaubriand and herb-rubbed rack of lamb—are one of the reasons Cypress has been awarded the local vote for "Most Romantic Restaurant." Save room for the made-to-order soufflé du jour.

82 Queen $$$ Lowcountry

82 Queen St. 843-723-7591. www.82queen.com.

Charleston's special-occasion restaurant for nearly 20 years is located in the heart of the Historic District. The restaurant's two connecting 19C row houses contain 11 romantic dining rooms. In nice weather, ask for a table in the charming courtyard, shaded by a towering magnolia tree. Award-winning she-crab soup, pan-fried McClellanville crab cakes, Southern Comfort BBQ shrimp and grits, and bourbon pecan pie highlight the restaurant's Lowcountry cuisine.

FIG
$$$ American

232 Meeting St., at Hassell St. Dinner only. Closed Sun. 843-805-5900. www.eatatfig.com.

Food is good at this Charleston newcomer—and that's coincidentally what FIG's name is an acronym for. Fresh seasonal fare steals the spotlight in the casual, understated dining room; think local white shrimp and chorizo, braised beef shortribs, Swiss chard ravioli. Take your pick of veggies for the table from the likes of potato purée, roasted beets and sautéed greens with garlic. Home-made desserts might include Fuji apple tart tatin, warm baked chocolate cake and espresso pana cotta. Don't come here in a hurry, though; all meals are carefully prepared to order at this member of Slow Food USA.

Fish
$$$ Seafood

442 King St. Closed Sun. 843-722-3474. www.fishrestaurant.net.

An 1837 single house is the setting for some great seafood in this upper King Street restaurant, set behind the Visitor Reception Center and next door to the American Theatre. Warm contemporary décor forms the backdrop for sensational seafood, such as grilled wreckfish (similar to snapper), sautéed grouper, whole fried flounder or seared North Carolina trout. Don't care for fancy sauces? Order the "naked" fresh fish of the day. On a politically correct note, the restaurant doesn't serve fish that are listed as endangered by the National Environment Trust and the Sustainable Seafood Education Project.

Fulton Five
$$$ Italian

5 Fulton St. Dinner only. Closed Sun. 843-853-5555.

Sage-green walls and crisp white tablecloths greet visitors to this cozy dining room, where Northern Italian fare rules. The seasonally changing menu might feature porcini-mushroom-rubbed beef filet with parmesan-polenta cake, or osso buco with whipped Yukon gold potatoes. The *pesce del giorno* (fish of the day) is a different preparation daily. Whatever's on the menu when you visit, one thing's for sure: high-quality imported ingredients—prosciutto, olive oil, fine cheeses and aged balsamic vinegar—make a meal here memorable.

Hank's Seafood Restaurant
$$$ Seafood

10 Hayne St. (at Church St.). Dinner only. 843-723-3474.

Hank's classy dining room has risen to local stardom since it appeared on the scene in 1999. After you whet your appetite with award-winning she-crab soup, crispy rock shrimp and calamari, or an oyster sampler from the raw bar, you'll have to choose between such tantalizing house specialties as roast grouper with caramelized onions and grain-mustard sauce, and a standout version of shrimp and grits—local shrimp, andouille sausage and stewed tomatoes atop creamy stone-ground grits.

J. Bistro
$$$ American

819 Coleman Blvd. (Rte. 703), Mt. Pleasant. Dinner only. Closed Mon. 843-971-7778. www.jbistro.net.

Carb-counters will welcome the bucket of veggie crudités that are brought to the table here in lieu of a big basket of bread (Okay, so there are rolls and flat-bread in the bucket, too, but you don't have to eat them). Located in sleepy Mt. Pleasant, J. Bistro surprises with its innovative fare. Decidedly Southern flair rules in Southern fried breast of chicken with chowchow or pecan-crusted catfish over creamy grits, while lobster won tons and sautéed shrimp in Thai red curry represent more global influences. Locals love the Sunday brunch.

Magnolias
$$$ Southern

185 E. Bay St. 843-577-7771. www.magnolias-blossom-cypress.com.

Chef Donald Barrickman classifies his menu here as "Uptown/Down South." That roughly translates to highbrow Southern food served in an upscale atmosphere, highlighted by wrought-iron elements and original artwork. Start with a bowl of the acclaimed Elwood's ham chowder, and move on to Carolina Carpetbagger filet with fried oysters, shellfish over grits, or coriander grilled yellowfin tuna. You won't find swordfish on the menu here, since Magnolias' staff supports the efforts being made to conserve all billfish species.

Peninsula Grill
$$$ New American

112 N. Market St., at the Planters Inn. Dinner only. 843-722-2345. www.peninsulagrill.com.

Acclaimed chef Robert Carter keeps them coming back with fabulous food and stellar service in his romantic dining room, accented with velvet-covered walls and warm-toned cypress woodwork. A crisp, cold wedge of iceberg lettuce topped with buttermilk dressing, or perhaps the generous trio of soups du jour, make good preludes to bourbon-grilled jumbo shrimp with Lowcountry hoppin' John and creamed corn, or seared sea scallops with toasted-pecan coulis. Peninsula Grill's signature dessert is the impossibly high—seven layers' worth—and scrumptious coconut cake, napped with coconut anglaise (talk about gilding the lily!). If you don't have room to try it after dinner, don't despair; the restaurant will be glad to ship one to you.

Rosebank Farms Café
$$$ Southern

Bohicket Marina Village, John's Island. 843-768-1807.

At this casual cafe facing the marina between Kiawah and Seabrook islands you'll find fresh seafood and local produce presented with classic southern accents. Veal meatloaf is grilled and served with fried green tomatoes; buttermilk-marinated, pan-seared chicken livers are paired with red-eye gravy and yellow hominy grits; and pan-roasted mahi-mahi is topped with Beaufort crabmeat. For dessert, the authentically tart Key lime pie tops the list. Try any of the Blue Plate specials for lunch.

Inexpensive

Basil $$ Thai

460 King St. 843-724-3490. www.basilthairestaurant.com.

If it's Thai food you crave, head for Basil, located on upper King Street at Ann Street. Be prepared to wait in line, though, since the popular eatery doesn't accept reservations. Even so, it's worth a wait for spicy green, red or masaman curries and other authentic dishes. Specialties include Pad Thai and red curry crispy duck—a deep-fried, boneless half-duck topped with vegetables and red curry sauce. Entrées are available with your choice of beef, chicken, pork, shrimp or tofu.

Gaulart & Maliclet $$ French

98 Broad St. Closed Sun. 843-577-9797. www.fastandfrench.org.

"Fast and French" is the motto of this small eatery, a favorite with Charleston's business lunchers. Pull up a stool at the communal counter and make a new friend; lunch specials include a glass of wine to promote the convivial atmosphere. For dinner, entrées range from seafood Normandy to beef Bordelaise to chicken provençal. There are "ethnic specials" on Friday and Saturday, and a selection of fondues on Thursday. Don't have time to stay? Most items here are available to take out.

Hominy Grill $$ Southern

207 Rutledge Ave. Open for breakfast, lunch & dinner Mon–Fri; dinner only on Sat; brunch Sun. 843-937-0930. www.hominygrill.com.

The staff at Hominy Grill believes you are what you eat. So they get their produce from area farms, their fish from local waters and their grits from a water-powered mill in North Carolina, near where chef Robert Stehling grew up. Hominy Grill may be a bit off the beaten path— it's located in an 1897 Charleston single house about 12 blocks outside the Historic District—but it's worth going out of your way for the likes of country-style pork ribs with red rice, shrimp creole with okra, and fried chicken with gravy and fluffy biscuits. Try a piece of fresh fruit pie or the creamy chocolate pudding for dessert.

Hyman's Seafood Company $$ Seafood

215 Meeting St. 843-723-6000. www.hymanseafood.com.

It seems there's always a line out the door at this popular seafood spot. And it's easy to see why— Hyman's orders fresh seafood daily and offers at least 15 choices on its menu board. Although they'll prepare your fish any way you like it (broiled, steamed, blackened, or even with Caribbean jerk seasoning), fried is clearly the preferred method. Can't decide? Go for one of the combo platters and make sure you include the crispy flounder, a house specialty. Save room for the Key lime pie.

Jestine's Kitchen $$ Southern

251 Meeting St., at the corner of Wentworth St. Closed Mon. 843-722-1541.

Looking for Southern soul food? You'll find it at this Charleston institution,
named for Jestine Matthews, who cared for the family of the restaurant's
founder and lived to be 112 years old. Wash down fried chicken, fried green
tomatoes, meatloaf or pecan-crusted whiting with Jestine's "table wine"—real
Southern sweet tea. For dessert, the Coca-Cola cake is the hands-down favorite.

39 Rue de Jean $$ French

39 John St. 843-722-8881. www.39ruedejean.com.

With its tin ceiling, exposed-brick walls and zinc bar,
this bustling brasserie looks—and tastes—French. Bistro
classics such as *steak frites* and *salade niçoise* share
menu space with a selection of sushi—an unexpected
addition. The more traditional chef's plats du jour
include braised short ribs, bouillabaise and coq au vin.
Steamed mussels (*moules*), a signature dish here, come
prepared six different ways; take your pick between
marinière, Brittany, pistou, curry, aioli, or vegetable
cream. The chocolate pâté is a popular dessert.

Baker's Café $ French

214 King St. Breakfast & lunch only. 843-577-2694. www.bakerscafe.com.

The menu here doesn't change much, but Baker's Café still packs 'em in for
Sunday brunch. In fact, you can get breakfast all day here; eleven different
poached-egg dishes are listed, along with croissant sandwiches, salads, pastas
and comfort-food casseroles. Entrées come with crusty French bread accompanied by whipped butter and raspberry jam. Choose a dessert from the display case filled with tempting homemade cakes and fruit tarts.

Kaminsky's $ Desserts

78 N. Market St. Open until 2am. 843-853-8270. www.tbonz.com.

You're sure to get your just desserts here. Right across
from the Old City Market, Kaminsky's is the locals' pick
for late-night dessert and coffee—or cordials and
single-malt scotch. A wide array of cakes and confec-
tions crowd the display case as you walk in. The wait
for a table allows time to narrow down your choices . . .
will it be Oreo cheesecake, bourbon pecan pie, or
caramel chocolate-chip pound cake?

Mosaic Café $ American

1150 Hungryneck Blvd., in Iron Gate Plaza, Mt. Pleasant. 843-888-1490.
www.mosaicedibles.com.

Just over the causeway from Isle of Palms, Mosaic offers creative, made-to-order
food to eat in or take out. Sandwiches and pizzas come on fresh pita bread,
stuffed with the likes of Buffalo chicken, roasted lamb or shrimp provençal. Salads
fill big bowls with crisp greens and a variety of other toppings such as gorgonzola
and walnuts, lamb and spinach or tarragon tuna. There's even a kids' menu.

Dining along the Grand Strand

Moderate

Collector's Cafe
$$$ Mediterranean

7726 N. Kings Hwy., Myrtle Beach. Dinner only. Closed Sun. 843-449-9370. www.collectorscafeandgallery.com.

Is it an art gallery or a restaurant? You be the judge. In fact, you can buy art *and* eat at Collector's Cafe, where hand-painting decorates tables, chairs and tiles, and original artwork blankets the walls. As for the food, pan-sautéed scallop cakes are served with tomato-scallion-garlic butter sauce; bone-in veal chop is pan-roasted with thyme demi-glace; and Sonoran-spiced yellowfin

tuna is grilled rare and topped with mango salsa. Between the ambience and the cuisine, it all combines to create a masterpiece of a restaurant.

Frank's Restaurant and Bar
$$$ International

10434 Ocean Hwy., Pawleys Island. Dinner only. Closed Sun. 843-237-3030. www.franksandoutback.com.

Named for the owner of a supermarket that once occupied this site, Frank's has been a local favorite since it opened in 1988. Seafood shines here, in such dishes as pan-fired grouper, sautéed shrimp and scallops, and fresh blackened catch of the day. Meat lovers will find much to satisfy them, too: roasted free-range chicken, pork tenderloin, veal scaloppini, New Zealand lamb. You'll even find some surprising touches from Asia and the Caribbean (crab spring rolls, Bahamian conch). If you're up for outdoor dining, try **Frank's Out Back ($$-$$$)**, where you can enjoy wood-fired pizzas or heartier entrées under tall

oaks. In crisp weather, there are infrared heaters and an outdoor fireplace to warm you; all year-round, there's live music on weekends.

Lee's Inlet Kitchen
$$$ Seafood

4460 Business 17, Murrells Inlet. 843-651-2881. www.leesinletkitchen.com.

Prices have hiked up a bit since Pearl and Eford Lee started their Murrells Inlet eatery in 1948. At that time, the seafood platter cost $1.50; now it's $19.95, but it still satisfies seafood lovers with a heaping portion of flounder, fantail shrimp, oysters, scallops and deviled crab (broiled or fried). And if that's not enough, your dinner comes with a salad, a choice of potato or vegetable, and fried hush puppies.

The Library $$$ Continental

*1212 N. Kings Hwy., Myrtle Beach. Dinner only. Closed Sun. 843-448-4527.
www.thelibraryrestaurantsc.com.*

With its tuxedoed waitstaff and traditional tableside preparations (Caesar salad, steak Diane, flambé desserts), The Library has been Myrtle Beach's special occasion restaurant since it opened its doors in 1974. Chateaubriand, duck à l'orange, chicken with artichokes, and salmon and shrimp *en papillote* are just a few of the selections that will tempt your tastebuds here.

Louis's at Pawleys $$$ Southern

*At the Hammock Shops, 10880 Ocean Hwy., Pawleys Island. 843-237-8757.
www.louisatpawleys.com.*

Charleston's loss is Pawleys' gain since Louis Osteen moved his restaurant from Meeting Street back to the island where he opened his first eatery. Chef and owner Louis Osteen, who won the James Beard award for Best Chef in the Southeast in 2004, dishes up Southern regional dishes such as Lowcountry she-crab soup, baby flounder with sweet-onion jam, fresh grilled fish, and a selection of steaks and chops. If it's more casual dining you're after, try the outdoor deck at adjacent **Louis's Fish Camp ($$)**, where strings of fish lights illuminate a lively bar scene, and the menu lists lighter fare—including Louis' signature crab and lobster cakes.

Phillips Seafood $$$ Seafood

*1807 21st Ave. N., Myrtle Beach. Dinner only. Call for off-season hours. 843-626-2722.
www.phillipsfoods.com.*

Born as Phillips Crab House in Ocean City, Maryland in 1956, this venerable seafood chain opened its Myrtle Beach outpost in 2003. Crab is king here, even though the menu lists a tempting selection of fried, broiled and grilled fish as well. The signature dish is the premium crab cakes, made with luscious all-lump crab meat, barely held together with mayonnaise and Phillips special seasonings. Other specialties include baked scallops stuffed with crab imperial, and the broiled seafood platter—a combo of the catch of the day, jumbo shrimp, scallops and a traditional crab cake.

Sea Captain's House $$$ American

3002 N. Ocean Blvd., Myrtle Beach. 843-448-8082. www.seacaptains.com.

This nautical-themed restaurant overlooking the Atlantic has a long history as a private beach cottage, and later as a guest house. Happily, it still welcomes guests who enjoy good food with an ocean view. Reasonably priced entrées (most under $20)—Lowcountry crab casserole, beer-battered shrimp, rib-eye steak, grilled chicken breast—come complete with a green salad or steamed veggies, hush puppies and your choice of potato, rice or French fries. The special children's menu makes this a good place for families.

Inexpensive

Hard Rock Cafe $$ American

Broadway on the Beach, US-17 at 21st Ave. N., Myrtle Beach. 843-946-0007.
www.hardrockcafe.com.

You can't miss the Hard Rock Cafe at
Myrtle Beach—it's shaped like an Egyptian
pyramid, complete with sphinxes guarding
the entrance. Inside, it's all-American,
though, from the burgers and barbecue to
the blaring old-time rock 'n roll. The décor
is rock memorabilia: guitars once played
by greats like the Allman Brothers, Jimi
Hendrix and Jerry Garcia line the walls,
along with tons of gold and platinum records honoring hits by everyone from
the Beatles to the Osmonds. Sure it's touristy, but the kids will want to go.

Island Café & Deli $$ Seafood

10683 Ocean Hwy., Pawleys Island. 843-237-9527. www.islandcafeanddeli.com.

Most customers like to eat outside under the awning, despite the constant
traffic on US-17. Huge fans here will keep you cool in summer. Monday night is
shrimp night; you'll get a pound of the Atlantic crustaceans, cooked any way
you like. On Tuesday and Wednesday the special is Maine lobster. Otherwise,
start with the fried alligator and move on to grouper with roasted red-pepper
cream sauce, or flounder with diced tomato and scallions over cheese grits.
End your meal with a little toe tapping to live music *(nightly)*.

Croissants Bakery & Cafe $ American

504-A 27th Ave. N., Myrtle Beach. Breakfast & lunch only. Closed Sun. 843-448-2253.
www.croissants.net.

Croissants makes a good place for that pre-golf
breakfast or lunchtime break from the sun. For lunch,
try the quiche of the day, the pimento cheese and
artichoke melt, or perhaps a Monte Cristo sandwich;
many of the deli sandwiches are served on fresh
croissants. Then sally up to the pastry case and drool
over the mouth-watering array of cakes and tortes.
You may just have to take one home with you!

Eggs Up Grill $ American

13088 Ocean Hwy., Pawleys Island. Breakfast & lunch only. 843-237-7313.
www.eggsupgrill.com.

Eggs any way—that's what you'll get at Eggs Up Grill, Pawleys' popular breakfast
haunt. Besides the basics, there's corned-beef hash and eggs, eggs Benedict, pancakes and eggs, steak and eggs . . . or customize your own three-egg omelet with
your choice of fillings. If you're not watching your carbs, try the French-toast pancakes, sprinkled with powdered sugar. An assortment of fresh sandwiches and
burgers rounds out the menu for lunch.

Dining along the Lowcountry Coast

Moderate

Michael Anthony's Cucina Italiana $$$ Italian

*37 New Orleans Rd., in Orleans Plaza, Hilton Head Island. Dinner only. Closed Sun.
843-785-6272. www.hiltonheaddlc.com/michaelanthony.htm.*

Authentic Italian food comes to Hilton Head at this popular restaurant, whose sleek dining room is done in warm wood tones and soft colors. Savor the likes of homemade potato gnocchi with fresh tomatoes and basil; filet mignon topped with mushrooms and Gorgonzola in a Barolo wine sauce; and veal saltimbocca (scaloppini of veal sautéed with white wine, garlic and veal demi-glaze, and blanketed with prosciutto and sage). For dessert, the signature tiramisu classico (ladyfingers soaked in espresso and rum, and layered with mascarpone mousse and cocoa) can't be beat.

Old Oyster Factory $$$ Seafood

*Marshland Rd., Hilton Head Island (1mi off Mathews Dr.). Dinner only. 843-681-6040.
www.oldoysterfactory.com.*

As you'd expect from a restaurant built on the site of one of Hilton Head's original oyster canneries, oysters come fresh from the local waters here. The island landmark features an open dining room with lots of floor-to-ceiling windows for views of Broad Creek and the surrounding marshland on three sides. Big appetites should go for the seafood medley, a platter piled high with fresh shrimp, scallops and local fish, plus oysters two ways (Savannah and Rockefeller), accompanied by rice and vegetables. Dieters can order any fish "naked," that is, grilled and brushed with olive oil and lemon juice.

Plums Waterfront Restaurant $$$ American

904 1/2 Bay St., Beaufort. 843-525-1946.

Plums' lively bistro atmosphere, with folk art adorning the walls, has been drawing local crowds since 1986. Try the Oyster Factory Creek shrimp roll, southern cousin of Maine's famed lobster rolls; the Beaufort version features local shrimp tossed with mayo, celery and spices on crusty French bread. Blue crab cakes, made with succulent lump crab meat, are another good bet. Listen to live music on Thursday, Friday and Saturday nights.

Red Fish $$$ Seafood

Palmetto Bay Rd., Hilton Head Island. 843-686-3388. www.redfishofhiltonhead.com.

On your way into Red Fish, stop at the restaurant's wine shop and pick up a bottle to complement the Cuban- and Caribbean-inspired fare, which ranges from Jamaican jerk shrimp to spicy Latin ribs with guava-orange barbecue sauce. Costa Rica rice pudding or warm tropical upside-down cake (guava sponge cake with pineapple, mango, kiwi and papaya) carry the exotic notes over to dessert. The real deal here is the early dining menu *(5pm–5:45pm)*: you'll get two courses, plus a beverage, for $13.95.

Saltus River Grill
$$$ Seafood

802 Bay St., Beaufort. Dinner only. 843-379-3474. www.saltusrivergrill.com.

This sophisticated spot over-looking the Intracoastal Waterway occupies the site of an 18C ship-yard; decorating the walls, photo-graphs mounted on sail canvas recall the building's past. You can't go wrong with specialties like grilled black grouper with roasted fennel and onions, sautéed sea bass and oysters with Pernod cream, and whole crispy fried flounder with warm pickled savoy cabbage. There's also a full sushi menu and an amazing list of oysters—the restaurant offers more than 60 types, from both the Atlantic and the Pacific.

Inexpensive

Brick Oven Cafe
$$ American

25 Park Plaza, Office Park Rd., Hilton Head Island. Dinner only. 843-686-2233.

At this casual eatery, gourmet pizzas—fired in the brick oven, of course—are definite winners, with a range of toppings from five cheeses (mozzarella, parmesan, feta, asiago and goat) to mesquite chicken to seafood marinara. Bring the family, or a crowd, and share tapas-like dishes of calamari or sweet-potato lobster cakes. There's something to please just about everyone's palate here; the extensive menu also features fresh fish, pastas and steaks (including a 23oz bone-in ribeye for hearty appetites!). Brick Oven Cafe caters to the young, late-night crowd with its smoking-optional policy and food service until 1am.

Shrimp Shack
$$ Seafood

1925 Sea Island Pkwy., St. Helena Island. Lunch Mon–Sat; dinner Fri & Sat only. Closed Sun. 843-838-2962.

Locals flock to this ultra-casual waterside eatery 15 minutes downwind of Beaufort, which has graced St. Helena Island for some 20 years. Probably the most popular item on the menu is their shrimp burger, but the crab cakes and flounder sandwiches are not far behind. Forget about that low-carb diet and go for the sweet-potato fries.

Blackstone's Cafe
$ American

205 Scott St., Beaufort. 843-524-4330. www.blackstonescafe.com. Breakfast & lunch only.

This favored breakfast and lunchtime gathering place emphasizes local seafood in its regional offerings. It's hard to top Blackstone's shrimp omelet and grits in the morning—stone-ground white and yellow grits are the house specialty. For midday meals, the homemade soups are much in demand. Sandwiches, salads and seafood dishes round out the menu. On a sunny day, you can enjoy the cafe's patio service.

Dining along the Georgia Coast

Moderate

CARGO Portside Grill $$$ American

*1423 Newcastle St., Brunswick. Dinner only. Closed Mon. 912-267-7330.
www.cargoportsidegrill.com.*

A ten-minute drive over the bridge from St. Simons or Jekyll Island will get you to the small, casual portside grill, whose décor reflects the history of Brunswick's busy port. Light on the bread crumbs, Cargo's crab cakes consistently win raves; other favorites include pasta Veracruz (linguine crowned with grilled chicken, poblano peppers, smoked tomatoes and caramelized onions in a Tequila-chipotle cream), and the half-pound Brunswick burger, topped with melted Maytag blue cheese, bacon and tobacco onions. Don't try to resist the Georgia peach pound cake, served hot off the griddle, with vanilla-bean ice cream and Jack Daniels caramel sauce.

Elizabeth on 37th $$$ New Southern

105 E. 37th St., Savannah. Dinner only. 912-236-5547. www.elizabethon37th.com.

Award-winning chef Elizabeth Terry works her gastronomic magic in a lovely Greek Revival-style mansion built for a wealthy cotton broker in the late 19C. Southern-fried grits with red-eye gravy and country ham, spicy Savannah red rice with Georgia shrimp, and honey-roasted pork tenderloin number among the mouth-watering menu choices. Terry accents her seasonal selections with herbs fresh from the restaurant's garden. Save room for the Savannah cream cake; it is as rich as it sounds.

The Lady & Sons $$$ Southern

102 W. Congress St., Savannah. 912-233-2600. www.ladyandsons.com.

Savannah native Paula Deen was newly divorced and unemployed when she started a catering business in town with her two sons in 1989. The successful endeavor grew into a restaurant, and today The Lady & Sons draws a loyal local following. Located in Savannah's historic City Market, the restaurant focuses on Southern home cooking. The dinner buffet features all-you-can-eat fried chicken, collard greens, creamed corn, rice and gravy—including salad and dessert—for $16.99. Or order crab cakes, French-cut pork chops, steaks and shrimp from the à la carte menu.

Sapphire Grill $$$ New American

110 W. Julian St., Savannah. Dinner only. 912-443-9962. www.sapphiregrill.com.

Fresh and seasonal cuisine is what you'll find at Sapphire Grill, a Savannah hot spot. Chef Christopher Nason hunts down dayboat scallops, local shrimp, heirloom vegetables, and USDA Prime beef for his seasonally changing menu. Sapphire bouillabaisse comes in a champagne shellfish bouillon; local black grouper is crusted with nutty benne seeds; and Colorado lamb chops are served on the bone as savory "lollipops." All this is served by an efficient staff against a background of stainless steel, exposed brick walls and original artwork in the chic dining room.

Must Eat: Georgia Coast Restaurants

Inexpensive

The Crab Shack $$ Seafood

40 Estill Hammock, Tybee Island. 912-786-9857. www.thecrabshack.com.

A former fish camp, this bare-bones eatery, located 17 miles east of Savannah on tiny Tybee Island, offers the freshest shellfish around. Huge portions of boiled or steamed crabs, shrimp and oysters come with corn on the cob and potatoes. You have to shell them yourself, though, so grab a roll of paper towels, pull up a bench at one of the wooden tables, and crack away. Buckets are provided for the shells.

SeaJay's Waterfront Cafe & Pub $$ Seafood

1 Harbor Rd., Jekyll Island. 912-635-3200. www.seajays.com.

Locals love this little cottage at Jekyll Harbor Marina for its Lowcountry boil buffet—an all-you-can-eat extravaganza of local shrimp, smoked sausage, corn on the cob and new potatoes for just $14.95. And, did we mention cole slaw, rolls and banana pudding for dessert? Dinner platters (shrimp scampi, crab cakes, broiled catch of the day) are served with rice and your choice of veg-etable or salad. SeaJay's original Brunswick Stew, soups, salads and sandwiches are available all day. Request a table outside for great water views.

B. Matthews Bakery ✳ $ American

325 E. Bay St., Savannah. 912-233-1319. www.bmatthewsbakery.com.

This downtown bakery tempts office workers with up to eight varieties of quiche and five different types of muf-fins for breakfast—and that's not to mention the bakery's yummy cinnamon rolls. Your best bet for lunch is one of the signature Southern sandwiches, all served on home-made wheatberry bread: black-eyed-pea cakes topped with pepper jack cheese; fried green tomatoes; or hickory-smoked bacon piled with fresh spinach, purple onion and gouda.

Gryphon Tea Room ✳ $ American

337 Bull St., at the corner of Charleton St., Savannah. 912-525-5880.

Breakfast and lunch are served in style at the Savannah School of Art & Design in a charming Old World setting of marble-topped bistro tables, crystal chan-deliers, stained glass and rich wood paneling. Light fare, such as the house salad (made with baby lettuces, artichoke hearts and walnuts topped with raspberry vinaigrette), three-egg omelets, and the Tea Set (scones, jam, fruit and tea) appeal to ladies who lunch. Tempting desserts fill the pastry case.

Vinnie Van Go-Go's ✳ $ Italian

317 W. Bryan St., on Franklin Square, Savannah. Open for dinner every day; lunch Sat & Sun. 912-233-6394. www.vinnievangogo.com.

It's not fancy, but locals and visitors alike crowd the indoor and outdoor tables at Vinnie's boisterous City Market location for tasty thin-crust New York-style pizza and generous calzones. Don't bother bringing your credit cards, though; Vinnie's only takes cash.

The properties listed below were selected for their ambience, location and/or value for money. Prices reflect the average cost for a standard double room for two people in high season. High season in Charleston and Savannah is in the spring and fall; rates are considerably lower in summer and winter. High season for the resort islands is in summer. Price ranges quoted do not reflect the South Carolina hotel tax of 12% or the Georgia hotel tax, which varies by county from 3% to 7%.

$$$$$	Over $350	$$	$100–$175
$$$$	$250–$350	$	Under $100
$$$	$175–$250		

Staying in the Charleston Area

Properties in this section are located in Charleston unless otherwise noted.

Luxury

Charleston Place Hotel $$$$$ 440 rooms

205 Meeting St. (main entrance off Hassell St.). 843-722-4900 or 800-611-5545. www.charlestonplacehotel.com.

A 3,000-piece Murano crystal chandelier hangs above the Georgian open-armed staircase in the elegant lobby of the grand dame of Charleston's hostelries, now operated by Orient Express Hotels, Inc. Renovated guest rooms are graciously appointed with 19C period furnishings, toile and floral patterns, and sumptuous marble baths. Amenities include a spa *(see Must Be Pampered)*, pool, fitness center, and the adjoining Charleston Place shopping mall. Your pet can enjoy dog or cat snacks from room service while you're downstairs savoring chef Bob Waggoner's innovative Southern cuisine at the hotel's renowned **Charleston Grill** *(see Must Eat)*.

The Sanctuary $$$$$ 255 rooms

1 Sanctuary Beach Dr., Kiawah Island. 843-768-6000 or 877-683-1234. www.thesanctuary.com.

Opened in August 2004, Kiawah's luxe new oceanfront hotel is everything you could want in a hotel. Designed to resemble a 19C seaside mansion, the hotel is flanked by 150-year-old transplanted live oaks on one side and the Atlantic Ocean on the other. Indeed, you'll feel like you're in someone's lavish living room as you step into the lobby, with its feminine morning room, 25-foot-high ceilings and ocean view. Room décor sports tones of gold and green; spacious marble baths have his-and-hers vanities and deep soaking tubs. Chill out on the beach or the palm-studded pool deck, or enjoy a treatment at the spa *(see Must Be Pampered)*. You'll savor New American cuisine at the formal **Ocean Room ($$$)**, or Lowcountry fare at clubby **Jasmine Porch ($$-$$$)**.

John Rutledge House Inn $$$$ 19 rooms

116 Broad St. 843-723-7999 or 866-720-2609. www.johnrutledgehouseinn.com.

A rough draft of the Constitution was written in this 1763 house, and resident John Rutledge was one of the 55 men who signed it. Inlaid parquet floors, canopied rice beds, carved plaster moldings and antiques and period reproductions typify this National Historic Landmark's restoration to its mid-18C appearance. A continental breakfast and evening wine and sherry come compliments of the house.

Market Pavilion Hotel $$$$ 66 rooms

225 E. Bay St. 843-723-0500 or 877-440-2250. www.marketpavilion.com.

This luxury property sits on the corner of East Bay and Market streets, right in the middle of the Historic District action; double-paned windows help screen out the noise. Your room will have its own foyer, mahogany furnishings, jewel-tone fabrics and elegant window treatments. You'll sleep in stylish comfort on Frette linens, with cashmere blankets and down pillows. Italian marble baths come equipped with fluffy towels and robes. Downstairs, **Grill 225 ($$$)** specializes in chop-house fare, while the rooftop **Pavilion Bar** *(see Musts for Fun)*, adjacent to the cascading pool, is a favorite local watering hole.

Must Stay: Charleston Area Hotels

Planters Inn $$$$ 62 rooms

112 N. Market St. 843-722-2345 or 800-845-7082. www.plantersinn.com.

The polished staff will greet you by name as you check into this charming Relais & Châteaux property, located on the bustling corner of Market and Meeting streets in the heart of the Historic District. Accommodations in the original 1844 building are designed in subtle colors with four-poster canopy beds, reproduction pieces and high ceilings; some rooms feature gas fireplaces. The building in back, added in 1997, carries over the vintage feel, with 21 rooms overlooking the courtyard's palm trees and fountains from a breezy loggia. A thoughtful touch: rooms are equipped with a white-noise machine to filter out the sound of nighttime revelry from Market Street. Be sure to sample the excellent contemporary American fare at the inn's **Peninsula Grill** *(see Must Eat)*.

Moderate

Charleston on the Beach Holiday Inn $$$ 132 rooms

1 Center St., Folly Beach. 843-588-6464 or 800-465-4329. www.charlestononthebeach.com.

Located at the end of Folly Road, the oceanfront Holiday Inn sits right in the center of the beach action (unlike other Charleston lodgings, their high season is summer). Newly renovated rooms all face the ocean with private balconies. You can rent nearly anything you need for recreation here, from umbrellas and chairs to jet skis, rafts, boogie boards and bicycles. Adults will favor the beachside Tiki Bar for frozen libations, while little ones will prefer Rockin' Robin's Ice Cream Shop. Kids under age 12 eat free here at Chancey's restaurant.

French Quarter Inn $$$ 50 rooms

166 Church St. 843-722-1900 or 866-812-1900. www.fqicharleston.com.

Champagne and ladyfinger cookies greet you at check-in at the French Quarter Inn, located just around the corner from Market Street. At night, you can slip into the triple-sheeted European bedding and choose your favorite among the seven different pillow selections on the inn's pillow menu. Amenities include afternoon wine and cheese, evening cookies and milk, turn-down service, and a gourmet continental breakfast delivered to your room. For business travelers, suites come complete with a computer, high-speed Internet access, a color printer and fax machine.

Fulton Lane Inn $$$ 27 rooms

202 King St. 843-720-2600 or 866-720-2940. www.charminginns.com.

Since Fulton Lane Inn is hidden on a tiny lane off King Street, you'll be spared some of the street noise from this busy commercial thoroughfare. King rooms have four-poster canopy beds, hardwood floors and white shuttered armoires; some feature fireplaces and whirlpool tubs. The friendly staff is happy to help you make restaurant reservations, arrange tours or supply information about the city's sights.

Governor's House Inn $$$ 12 rooms

117 Broad St. 843-720-2070 or 800-720-9812. www.governorshouseinn.com.

When Governor Edward Rutledge lived here in the late 1700s, this lovely mansion, with its crystal chandeliers, nine fireplaces and double piazza (as porches are called in Charleston), entertained lots of local notables. Now you can stay here, equally close to The Battery and to the shops, restaurants and galleries of the Historic District. Individually decorated rooms are richly outfitted with period furnishings, fresh flowers and hardwood floors; many boast private porches, fireplaces and whirlpool baths. Amenities include free on-site parking (rare in the Historic District), a continental breakfast, afternoon tea and evening sherry.

Hampton Inn Historic District $$$ 171 rooms

345 Meeting St. 843-723-4000 or 800-426-7866. www.hamptoninn.com.

Adjacent to the Charleston Visitor Reception Center and across the street from the Charleston Museum, this 19C railroad warehouse now welcomes guests in its incarnation as a Hampton Inn. Clean, comfortable rooms sport an antebellum décor, with mahogany furnishings and floral prints. Public areas boast pine floors and Oriental carpets. Besides its convenient location, the hotel offers a pool, free local calls, and a complimentary breakfast bar.

Harbour View Inn $$$ 52 rooms

2 Vendue Range. 843-853-8439 or 888-853-8439. www.harbourviewcharleston.com.

Adjacent to Waterfront Park, this family-friendly Historic District property overlooks Charleston Harbor. The lobby area, with its breezy island-inspired décor, recalls the days when many of Charleston's residents hailed from the Caribbean. Lowcountry-style guest rooms feature 14-foot ceilings, four-poster beds draped with matelassé coverlets, wicker furnishings and seagrass rugs. Many rooms have harbor views. Rates include a continental breakfast delivered to your room or served in the lobby, afternoon wine and cheese, all-day snacks and iced tea, fresh-baked cookies and milk in the evening, and turn-down service.

The Inn at Middleton Place $$$ 53 rooms

4300 Ashley River Rd., at Middleton Place Plantation. 843-556-6020 or 800-782-3608. www.middletonplace.org.

You're sure to feel close to nature at the Inn at Middleton Place. Rooms here, located on the grounds of Middleton Place Plantation *(see Plantations),* are done in a warm contemporary style designed to take advantage of the inn's lovely surroundings—think floor-to-ceiling windows with plantation shutters, cypress paneling, handmade furnishings and braided rugs. For the price of a room, you'll enjoy a full breakfast in the Lake House, an evening wine and hors d'oeuvres reception, an in-room refrigerator stocked with snacks, and unlimited access to bicycles for exploring the grounds. The best part: you'll receive free passes to Middleton Place Gardens, the House Museum and the Stableyards.

Mills House Hotel $$$ 214 rooms

115 Meeting St. 843-577-2400 or 800-874-9600. www.millshouse.com.

This property has nearly everything you could ask for in a moderately priced hotel: an outdoor pool and sundeck, a cozy courtyard, two bars, the Barbadoes Room Restaurant (try their Sunday brunch), and a Grand Ballroom for those special occasions—and it's all set on Meeting Street, in the heart of the Historic District. Well-appointed rooms boast period furnishings and come with nightly turn-down service. On the private-access executive level, the room rate includes plush robes, a continental breakfast and evening hors d'oeuvres.

Two Meeting Street Inn $$$ 9 rooms

2 Meeting St. 843-723-7322. www.twomeetingstreetinn.com.

What a treat to stay at the tip of The Battery, in this stunning 19C home overlooking the water! Sister property to the Governor's House Inn, Two Meeting Street is known for the gracious Southern hospitality of its innkeepers. The Queen Anne Victorian was built for newlyweds Waring and Martha Carrington in 1890. Inside, its gleaming English oak woodwork, Tiffany stained-glass windows and crystal chandeliers bespeak the considerable means of the wealthy couple. Rooms have four-poster beds, most with lacy canopies. Ask the concierge to make dinner reservations and arrange for sightseeing tours or theater tickets.

Vendue Inn $$$ 65 rooms

19 Vendue Range. 843-577-7970 or 800 845-7900. www.vendueinn.com.

Carved out of several 18C warehouses, the Vendue Inn is a Charleston classic. No two rooms here are alike, but all are adorned with antiques and 18C reproductions. In some rooms, reproduction wallpaper and brick walls add historic charm, while marble baths and Jacuzzi tubs provide modern luxury. All rooms furnish fluffy robes, safes, air- and water-purification systems, and evening turn-down service. Rates include a buffet breakfast, milk and cookies before bed and use of bicycles for cruising the Historic District. Try New American cuisine at **The Library ($$$)** or light fare upstairs at the popular **Roof Top Bar and Restaurant** *(see Musts for Fun).*

Wentworth Mansion $$$ 24 rooms

149 Wentworth St. 843-853-1886 or 888-466-1886. www.wentworthmansion.com.

A bit off the beaten track, but still in the Historic District, Wentworth Mansion envelops guests in opulent surroundings—think hand-carved marble fireplaces, Tiffany stained-glass windows, rich woodwork—in quarters built for a wealthy cotton merchant in 1886. Roomy chambers have king-size beds, gas fireplaces, hardwood floors and whirlpool tubs; some feature daybeds for extra guests. Start your day here with a complimentary European breakfast buffet served on the airy sunporch. Then relax by the fireplace in the parlor, curl up with a book in the library, or treat yourself to a session in the Wentworth's new spa. Your taste buds will be delighted by the New American fare served at the on-site **Circa 1886** restaurant **($$$).**

Inexpensive

Andrew Pinckney Inn $$ 41 rooms

40 Pinckney St. 843-937-8800 or 800-505-8983. www.andrewpinckneyinn.com.

You can't go wrong for the price at the Andrew Pinckney Inn, conveniently located two blocks from the Old City Market. The original 1840 structure was renovated in 2001, at which time the inn added six rooms and three town-house suites in a new building across the street. Enjoy a complimentary continental breakfast on the rooftop terrace, while you scope out the sights.

The Ashley Inn $$ 7 rooms

201 Ashley Ave. 843-723-1848 or 800-581-6658. www.charleston-sc-inns.com.

Guests at this two-story gabled house, built in 1832, can take full advantage of the airy double piazzas cooled by ceiling fans. Rooms in the residential B&B are tastefully appointed with traditional furnishings, including canopy, four-poster or pencil-post beds; all have private bathrooms and cable TV. Start a busy day of sightseeing with the orange croissant French toast, or sausage turnovers with cream-cheese-and-chive scrambled eggs (included in the rate).

Boardwalk Inn $$ 93 rooms

Palmetto Dr. at Wild Dunes, Isle of Palms. 843-886-6000 or 888-778-1876. www.wilddunes.com.

If you don't want to rent a place for a whole week at Wild Dunes resort, the Boardwalk Inn is a great option. You'll still have access to all the resort's amenities, which include a fitness center, tennis courts, and two award-winning golf courses *(see p 91)*. When you're not relaxing in your balconied room with its sand and coral palette, you can pedal along the bike paths, swim in the pools, or just lie on the beach.

Indigo Inn $$ 40 rooms

1 Maiden Lane. 843-577-5900 or 800-845-7639. www.indigoinn.com.

Built in the mid-19C as a warehouse to store indigo, this building was converted into a bed-and-breakfast inn in 1979. Today the Indigo Inn, located a block away from the Old City Market, lodges guests in rooms decorated with Colonial-style furnishings, some with four-poster rice beds. Most rooms overlook the pretty brick courtyard, with its greenery and inviting hot tub. In the morning, enjoy a complimentary breakfast of assorted breads, ham biscuits and fruit.

The Westin Francis Marion $$ 226 rooms

387 King St. 843-722-0600 or 877-756-2121. www.francismarioncharleston.com.

Named for Revolutionary War hero Francis Marion (aka the "Swamp Fox"), this hotel premiered in 1924 at the corner of Calhoun and King streets, near shopping, restaurants, and the College of Charleston. Restored in 1996, the 12-story hotel encloses rooms with high ceilings and dark-wood furniture. A visit to the downstairs **Spa Adagio** *(see Must Be Pampered)* will massage away your tension.

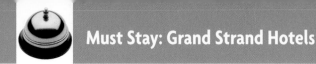
Staying along the Grand Strand

Luxury

Litchfield Plantation $$$$ 38 rooms

Kings River Rd., Litchfield Beach. 843-237-9121 or 800-869-1410. www.litchfieldplantation.com.

Gone With The Wind may come to mind as you you enter the wrought-iron gates of this former rice plantation, with its quarter-mile avenue of Spanish moss-draped live oaks leading to the c.1750 white-columned mansion. Distinctive accommodations range from deluxe rooms to executive suites, all with access to fully equipped kitchens. Litchfield Plantation isn't on the beach, but guests have access to an exclusive ocean-front clubhouse on Pawleys Island. Dinner at the **Carriage House Club ($$$)** features continental classics as well as Lowcountry fare.

Moderate

The Breakers Resort Hotel $$$ 238 rooms in the hotel
540 units total in the resort

Ocean Blvd. at N. 21st Ave., Myrtle Beach. 843-444-4444 or 800-952-4507. www.breakers.com.

The Breakers has been a Myrtle Beach landmark for 70 years. Standard hotel rooms, most with balconies and many with microwaves and refrigerators, are done in light woods and tropical hues. Need larger lodgings? Try one of the two towers that have been added to the property; they feature one-, two- and three-room suites, and spacious condominiums. No matter which locale you choose, the kids will love the oceanfront water park.

Evans Pelican Inn $$$ 9 rooms

506 Myrtle Ave., Pawleys Island. 843-237-2298. www.evanspelicaninn.com.

Owned by the Evans family since 1970, the weatherbeaten wood-frame inn now attracts guests seeking casual comfort and laid-back charm. Upstairs accommodations are simply furnished and cooled by ceiling fans (the inn has no air-conditioning); three rooms have private baths. An enclosed wraparound porch, a tree-shaded boardwalk to the beach, and a family-style breakfast are all guest pleasers.

Hampton Inn, Broadway at the Beach $$$ 141 rooms

1140 Celebrity Circle, Myrtle Beach. 843-916-0600 or 888-916-2001. www.hamptoninn.com.

If you don't mind being off the beach, consider this Hampton Inn, at the heart of the 350-acre entertainment complex Broadway at the Beach *(see p 131)*. Tons of shops, restaurants, mini-golf, Ripley's Aquarium *(see p 126)* and many other amusements will be right outside your door. You'll also be treated to standard Hampton amenities such as free local calls and a complimentary breakfast bar.

Sea View Inn $$$ 20 rooms

414 Myrtle Ave., Pawleys Island. 843-237-4253. www.seaviewinn.net. (Room rate includes three meals a day.) Open late-Mar–late Nov.

Step outside the rambling, two-story Sea View Inn and you're literally on the beach—the inn's private beach. That, plus a friendly staff, delicious meals, and the absence of phones and TVs, lure guests to this oceanfront hostelry, in business since 1937. You won't find air-conditioning or in-room baths here, but you will find rocking chairs on the porch, good books in the living room and lots of friendly conversation.

Inexpensive

Anderson Inn $$ 111 rooms

2600 N. Ocean Blvd., Myrtle Beach. 843-448-1535 or 800-437-7376. www.andersoninn.com.

This family-owned inn, set on the ocean in the middle of Myrtle Beach, offers clean, no-frills lodging. Amenities such as refrigerators in all rooms appeal to families, as do efficiencies and kitchen rooms with microwaves and coffee-makers. Then there's the fitness room, Jacuzzi, and indoor and outdoor pools. Little ones will appreciate the shallow oceanfront pool that's just for kids.

Beach Colony Resort $$ 218 units

5308 N. Ocean Blvd., Myrtle Beach. 843-449-4010 or 800-222-2141. www.beachcolony.com.

Come by yourself, or bring a crowd; Beach Colony offers oceanfront suites, studio rooms with kitchenettes, and one-, two-, three- and four-bedroom condominiums. Take a dip in one of the indoor or outdoor pools, soak in the whirlpools, sip a drink at the oceanfront lounge or play a game of racquetball in the resort's court. All this, plus a lazy river tubing ride and a video arcade for the kids.

Ocean Creek Plantation Resort $$ 750 units

10600 N. Kings Hwy., North Myrtle Beach. 843-272-7724 or 877-844-3800. www.oceancreek.com.

A full-service resort, Ocean Creek Plantation offers accommodations from lodge efficiencies to three-bedroom oceanfront units. There's a restaurant, a sand volleyball court, a putting green, a separate pool and playground for the kiddies, and a tram to ferry guests to and from the beach. Units are tastefully decorated with colors inspired by the sand and surf, just outside.

Staying along the Lowcountry Coast

Luxury

Inn at Palmetto Bluff $$$$$ 58 rooms

476 Mt. Pelia Rd., Bluffton. 843-706-6500 or 866-706-6565. www.palmettobluffresort.com.

Newest of the Auberge Resorts (the people who brought you Auberge du Soleil in Napa Valley, California), the Inn at Palmetto Bluff caters to sybarites with a host of high-end amenities. The smallest rooms here are 1,140-square-foot cottages, outfitted with heart-pine floors, fireplaces, steam showers, and screened-in porches, for a start. That's not to mention wet bars, plasma TVs, Sub-Zero refrigerators, and DVD/CD players. Village homes, which come with two, three or four bedrooms, are perfect for families. Oh, and did we mention the **May Riverhouse** restaurant (**$$$$**) with its fine Lowcountry cuisine, the serene spa *(see Must Be Pampered)* and the 18-hole Jack Nicklaus-designed golf course? All this is set on 20,000 acres of lovely marshland and forest bordering the May River.

Moderate

Disney's Hilton Head Island Resort $$$ 123 rooms

22 Harbourside Lane, Hilton Head Island. 843-341-4100 or 800-695-8284. http:/dvc.disney.go.com.

Designed to look like a rustic hunting lodge, along the lines of Disney World's Wilderness Lodge in Orlando, this Disney resort has a laid-back feel. It's not on the beach, but the resort does own a private beach house that you can reach via the hotel's shuttle. Choose from studios, or one-, two- and three-bedroom villas, the latter outfitted with full kitchens. As you'd expect from Disney, there are lots of activities for all members of the family, from the Tot Lot playground to teen kayaking and family fishing adventures.

Inn at Harbour Town $$$ 60 rooms

7 Lighthouse Lane, Hilton Head Island. 843-363-8100 or 888-807-6873. www.seapines.com.

Casual elegance will envelope you as you enter this sophisticated property, located near the Harbour Town Yacht Basin at Sea Pines Plantation. Rooms are custom designed in crisp colors with marble baths, soaking tubs and cotton Frette linens. Harbour Town Golf Links and the Sea Pines Racquet Club are just outside your door, and a short walk will bring you to the shops and restaurants of Harbour Town itself. The inn's accommodating staff of English butlers are available around the clock to cater to your every need, from sending faxes to pressing clothes.

Main Street Inn $$$ 33 rooms

2200 Main St., Hilton Head Island. 843-681-3001 or 800-471-3001. www.mainstreetinn.com.

Luxury comes at a reasonable price at this Hilton Head inn. Modeled after a European boutique hotel, the Main Street Inn wraps guests in cushy comfort with brocade fabrics, Second Empire-style furnishings, and Frette robes. Luxury

double rooms boast spacious baths, upscale linens and ceiling fans; some queen rooms have fireplaces, and roomy courtyard kings overlook a gurgling fountain. You may even be tempted to forego that golf game in favor of languishing by the pool, surrounded by fragrant gardenias. Rates include a full American breakfast served in the sunny dining room, turn-down service and afternoon tea.

Rhett House Inn $$$ 18 rooms

1009 Craven St., Beaufort. 843-524-9030 or 888-480-9530. www.rhetthouseinn.com.

The inviting double veranda of the Rhett House Inn beckons guests to this gracious lodging. Rooms are decked out individually in fabrics ranging from feminine pink florals to sophisticated black-and-white toile; many have four-poster beds. Stay to meet some of your fellow inn-mates during afternoon tea or evening wine and hors d'oeuvres. French toast, pancakes or eggs and grits are likely to greet you at the breakfast table. Whether you choose to wander Beaufort's historic district or sunbathe at nearby Hunting Island State Park, Rhett House makes a great base for exploring the area. Of course, you might just as well simply settle back on the inn's shady front porch and watch the world go by.

Inexpensive

The Beaufort Inn $$ 21 rooms

809 Port Republic St., Beaufort. 843-521-9000. www.beaufortinn.com.

Hospitality shines in this 1897 mansion in historic downtown Beaufort, which has entertained the likes of Julia Roberts and CBS news anchor Paula Zahn. Each guest room is so uniquely decorated, you could stay in a different one every night and never get bored. Styles range from rich, dark Victorian to cotton-candy pastels with hand-painted furniture. Some rooms have wet bars; some have fireplaces; all teem with Southern charm. A full American breakfast and afternoon tea are part of the package. The inn's formal **dining room ($$$)** stands on its own merits, de-lighting diners with Lowcountry fare ranging from fresh seafood to steak.

South Beach Marina Inn $$ 17 rooms

232 South Sea Pines Dr., Hilton Head Island. 843-671-6498 or 800-367-3909. www.southbeachvillage.com.

Located in Sea Pines Plantation, this inn tucks into a New England-style village complex of shops and restaurants. Accommodations, which are done in country décor and include one- and two-bedroom units, all have kitchenettes—making them ideal for families. The Atlantic Ocean lies just a few minutes' walk away, and guests here have access to Sea Pines amenities such as golf, tennis, watersports and bike trails.

Staying along the Georgia Coast

Luxury

The Cloister $$$$$ 249 rooms

100 Salt Marsh Lane, Sea Island. 912-638-3611 or 800-732-4752. www.seaisland.com.

Built by renowned Florida architect Addison Mizner, The Cloister has graced Georgia's Golden Isles since 1928. Today the original 75-year old Cloister Hotel is undergoing a $200 million renovation, scheduled to be completed in spring 2006. For now, guests can still stay at the Lodge, overlooking the Plantation golf course, and at the Ocean Houses, all of which have access to five miles of private beach. While the kids are occupied with organized resort activities, you can escape to the Sea Island Spa *(see Must Be Pampered)*, play a around of golf, or hit the tennis courts.

Greyfield Inn $$$$$ 17 rooms

On Cumberland Island. Ferry transportation to the inn runs from Fernandina Beach, Florida. Two-night minimum stay. 904-261-6408. www.greyfieldinn.com.

This is where you want to go when you *really* need to get away; the inn, accessible by boat, is the only commercial establishment on the island. Built in 1900 *(see p 160)*, Greyfield provides access to the secluded reaches of Cumberland Island National Seashore. Rooms (some with shared baths) are decorated with Carnegie family heirlooms and antiques. Rates include three meals a day and unlimited use of bicycles and sports, fishing and beach equipment. Note that there's no phone service or transportation on the island.

The Gastonian $$$$ 17 rooms

220 E. Gaston St., Savannah. 912-232-2869 or 800-322-6603. www.gastonian.com.

Attentive service defines Southern hospitality in the two adjoining Regency-style mansions that house this luxurious historic district inn. All guest quarters have working fireplaces and are elegantly appointed with Oriental rugs and antique four-poster, iron or carved wood beds. Many come with whirlpool tubs. For breakfast, you'll be hard-pressed to choose from a menu of tasty entrées that includes lemon cheese pancakes with strawberry glaze, a fruit and yogurt plate, and made-to-order omelets.

Moderate

Eliza Thompson House $$$ 25 rooms

5 W. Jones St., Savannah. 912-236-3620 or 800-348-9378. www.elizathompsonhouse.com.

Named for the society widow who built the stately house in 1847, this lovely B&B sits on a quiet residential street in Savannah's historic district. Rooms, each one unique, are decked out in rich colors with four-poster or canopy beds and antique furnishings. You certainly won't go hungry here: room rates include a a deluxe buffet breakfast in the courtyard, an evening wine and cheese reception, and desserts and coffee before bedtime. Spend a few hours in the pretty courtyard listening to the burbling fountain. Another extra: guests receive a pass for the metered street parking.

Jekyll Island Club Hotel $$$ 157 rooms

371 Riverview Dr., Jekyll Island. 912-635-2600 or 800-535-9547. www.jekyllclub.com.

Completed in 1902 as a hunting retreat for America's monied elite *(see p 158)* this restored National Historic Landmark retains its turn-of-the-century charm. The renovated historic Crane (1917) and Cherokee (1904) cottages offer additional luxurious rooms and suites. With three 18-hole golf courses, nine tennis courts, and a beach club nearby (free shuttle service is provided for guests), you may never want to leave the family-friendly complex. Save a night for dinner in the lavish Victorian **Grand Dining Room ($$$)**, which specializes in regional cuisine.

Mulberry Inn $$$ 145 rooms

601 E. Bay St., Savannah. 912-238-1200 or 877-468-1200. www.savannahhotel.com.

This historic hotel was built as a livery stable in 1860. Overlooking Washington Square in Savannah's historic district, the Mulberry Inn features traditional-style rooms newly renovated in dark woods and rich hunt colors. If you're planning a longer stay, consider one of the deluxe rooms, which have VCRs, refrigerators and microwaves. Afternoon tea and pastries, a fitness room, and a pool and hot tub number among the amenities here. The on-site Sgt. Jasper's Tavern makes a cozy setting for an evening cocktail.

Inexpensive

Bed and Breakfast Inn $$ 15 rooms

117 W. Gordon St., Savannah. 912-238-0518 or 888-238-0518. www.savannahbnb.com.

OK, so the name's not very creative, but according to the owners, this historic district hostelry on Chatham Square was the first B&B in Savannah, opened in 1978. Air-conditioned rooms all have queen or four-poster beds, private baths, TVs, and bonuses like irons and ironing boards and hair dryers. Rates include a full breakfast and afternoon tea. Downsides: Parking is on the street, and it's metered; a two-night minimum is required on weekends.

Green Palm Inn $$ 5 suites and a 2-bedroom cottage

548 E. President St., Savannah. 912-447-8901 or 888-606-9510. www.greenpalminn.com.

This 1897 Victorian houses guests in comfort in its suites, outfitted with British Colonial-style furnishings to play on Savannah's British heritage. Each suite is individually decorated: the Royal Palm boasts two fireplaces, including one in the bathroom; the Cottage Palm suite has a gourmet kitchen and its own private entrance. Guests at the Green Palm are treated to a full hot breakfast each morning and refreshments in the afternoon. The staff will be glad to recommend restaurants, make dinner reservations and arrange for city tours.

Index

The following abbreviations may appear in this Index: GA Georgia; SC South Carolina; NHP National Historical Park; NHS National Historic Site; NRA National Recreation Area; SHP State Historic Park; SHS State Historic Site; SP State Park.

Index

Photo Credits:

YOUR OPINION MATTERS!

Thank you for purchasing a Michelin Travel Publications product. To help us continue to offer you the absolute best in travel guides, maps and atlases, we need your feedback.

Please fill in this questionnaire and return it to:
Michelin Travel Publications – Attn: Marketing
P.O. Box 19001
Greenville, SC 29602-9001, USA

To thank you, we will draw one name from the returned questionnaires each month from January 2005 to year end. Each month's winner will receive a free 2005 North America Road Atlas (retail value: $17.95 US/ $19.95 CAN).

1. How would you rate the following features of the product, if applicable?
  1 = *Very Good*   **2** = *Acceptable*   **3** = *Poor*

	1	2	3
Selection of attractions/sights	❏	❏	❏
Practical Information (prices, etc.)	❏	❏	❏
Description of establishments	❏	❏	❏
General presentation	❏	❏	❏
Cover	❏	❏	❏

2. How satisfied were you with this product?

❏ Very satisfied ❏ Satisfied ❏ Somewhat Satisfied ❏ Not Satisfied

If not satisfied, how should we improve the product? _____

_____

3. Did you buy this product: *(check multiple if necessary)*
  ❏ For holiday/vacation
  ❏ For short breaks or weekends
  ❏ For business purposes
  ❏ As a gift
  ❏ Other

4. Where would you buy and expect our products to be available?
  (check multiple if necessary)

  ❏ Supermarket   ❏ Mass Merchandiser (Costco, Sam's, etc.)
  ❏ Convenience store ❏ Specialty store (museum shop, travel store, etc.)
  ❏ Bookstore   ❏ Gas/Service Station
  ❏ Online   ❏ Kiosk/Gift shop

5. Which destinations do you visit the most often for pleasure? *(list as many locations as you wish)* _____

_____

MSCC05

6. Which destinations do you visit the most often for business? *(list as many locations as you wish)* _____

_____

7. When you go on vacation, generally how long do you stay?
(check multiple if necessary)
- ❏ Three or four days
- ❏ One week
- ❏ Two weeks
- ❏ A combination of short (three or four days) and one week vacations
- ❏ Other _____

8. When you travel, what mode of transportation do you most frequently use?
(1 – most frequent, 6 – least frequent)

____**Plane** ____**Car** ____**Bus** ____**Train** ____**Cruise** ____**Other**

9. Would you consider buying other Michelin travel books or products?

❏ Yes ❏ No

If yes, which one(s):

- ❏ Must SEES
- ❏ North America 2005 Road Atlas
- ❏ North America Regional Road Atlas + Travel Guide
- ❏ North America Regional Road Atlas
- ❏ North America Regional Maps
- ❏ Green Guide (North American titles)
- ❏ Green Guide (European titles)
- ❏ Red Guide
- ❏ European City Maps
- ❏ Other_____

10. Your age?
- ❏ Less than 25 years old
- ❏ 25–35 years old
- ❏ 36–45 years old
- ❏ 46–55 years old
- ❏ 56–65 years old
- ❏ 65 years plus

11. May we be of assistance to you in any way?

_____

_____

Telephone or e-mail where we may reach you: _____

If you would like to be added to our mailing list, please fill out the information below:

❏ **Ms.** ❏ **Mrs.** ❏ **Mr.**

Name _____

Address _____

City_____ State _____

Zip Code_____ Country_____

E-mail, if you would like to receive an electronic update from us:

_____